Five Centuries
of American
Costume

Five Centuries of American Costume

R. Turner Wilcox

ILLUSTRATED

DOVER PUBLICATIONS, INC.
Mineola, New York

Bibliographical Note

This Dover edition, first published in 2004, is an unabridged republication of
the work originally published in 1963 by Charles Scribner's Sons, New York.

Library of Congress Cataloging-in-Publication Data

Wilcox, R. Turner (Ruth Turner), 1888-
    Five centuries of American costume / R. Turner Wilcox.
        p. cm.
    Originally published: New York : Charles Scribner's Sons, 1963.
    Includes bibliographical references.
    ISBN 0-486-43610-1 (pbk.)
      1. Clothing and dress—United States—History. I. Title.

GT605.W5W55 2004
391'.00973—dc22

2004043929

Manufactured in the United States of America
Dover Publications, Inc., 31 East 2nd Street, Mineola, N.Y. 11501

To Ray and Ruth Wilcox

FOREWORD

THIS WORK WAS UNDERTAKEN upon the suggestion of my publishers who wished a book on American everyday costume covering that of the American Indians, the European warriors who followed Columbus and the civilians who eventually came to stay and build in the New World. What at first seemed almost too ambitious a project finally resolved itself into a pattern. The story has been worked out principally in illustrations founded upon research, the execution of which proved to be exciting, absorbing and rewarding.

The subject might appear in light vein to some but it is a study that leads deep into antiquity, history and the art of all peoples. For instance, it was fascinating to begin with the American Indians and their tattooing. There were not always garments to wear but some form of body decoration has always been eagerly sought and has always been found. In that ever-present desire to decorate the human form, man has succeeded by taking from nature, flowers, furs, horns and so forth, even by mutilation of the flesh as in tattooing and reshaping some parts of the body as the ears, nose and mouth, despite the pain incurred. Instances of pain and discomfort continue to be endured for vanity's sake even in our supposedly enlightened day and age. So the spirit of dress has not changed down the ages.

The American way of life has evolved a way of dressing which is pure Americana. Simple, comfortable and wherewithal smart, it is appropriate for any hour of day or evening where full dress is not specified. It is attractive enough for other peoples to wish to copy and therein lies the proof of its adaptability. "Casual dress" is the predominant note of our everyday dress and that is what we have tried to portray in our book.

Any dress of any people anywhere in the world is a possible inspiration in the design of costume. With that thought in mind I present this collection of historic everyday apparel to all those interested and working in so vital a subject as dress costume.

R.T.W.

Tenafly, New Jersey
1962

CONTENTS

CONTENTS

CONTENTS

xiii

CONTENTS

CHAPTER TEN

CHILDREN—16TH TO 20TH CENTURIES   183

16TH AND 17TH CENTURIES

18TH CENTURY

19TH CENTURY

20TH CENTURY

CONTENTS

THE EARLIEST SETTLERS IN AMERICA

CHAPTER ONE

THE FIRST WHITE MEN to reach the American continent were the Norsemen or Northmen who called themselves Vikings, piratical sea-rovers from the Scandinavian Lands. From the eighth to the eleventh centuries they ranged over the northern ocean reaching America by way of Iceland and Greenland. Bold, courageous and capable shipbuilders, but terrifying warriors, they went in quest of fertile lands and plunder. Their New World discoveries included Labrador, Newfoundland, Cape Breton and Nova Scotia or Vinland where attempts were made to colonize and then abandoned, why, we do not know. The Scandinavian adventures were not collected and recorded in writing until the thirteenth century.

They found the continent peopled with a swarthy race, ugly and ferocious looking. "Weaklings" the invaders called them. Bartering took place but there was also quarreling which was no doubt the reason for relinquishing any further attempt at settlements. Whence the aborigines came or how they came is a moot question but it is fairly well conceded that they reached our shores by way of Siberia and Bering Strait. By the time the European explorers arrived the settlements of these Asiatics or Mongolians were to be found on both continents reaching from the Arctic coast to Tierra del Fuego, having fanned southward adapting themselves to climate and terrain.

Those who settled in the Arctic region became known as Eskimos, a term meaning "those who eat raw flesh" but their name for themselves was "Innuit" or "the people." Knowledge of their early history is vague but the speech is akin to the primitive American Indian dialects and their customs and legends resemble those of the Indians. The Eskimos are a short, stocky people with round, broad faces, narrow eyes and coarse, jet black hair.

Dress for both men and women has always been of skins furnished by seal, reindeer, bear, dog or fox. The intense cold necessitates a fitted, tailored outfit for both sexes with fur breeches tucked into fur boots, a hooded tunic or parkeh, the hood of the woman's garment being large enough in which to carry a baby. Wolverine, to which frost does not adhere, edges the hood. Two parkehs are worn in the winter, one with the fur outside and the other with the fur next to the body. Formerly the well-fitted suits were beautifully sewn with sinew thread and bone needle. Basically, costume has not changed but modern Eskimo dress is more elaborate in cut and colorfully ornamented with beaded and cut-out motifs.

The Indians of the North Pacific coast were the creators of art works now considered to be the highest form of North American Indian art in their remarkable totem poles, costumes and masks for the dance, the working of native copper and silver and beautiful weaving of basketry. Because of the mild climate they went barefoot the year round, in the rainy season taking to a raincoat in the form of a poncho of cedar bark. Though some old men went about naked, young men always wore the breechclout held up by a string belt. The woman's apron of cedar bark was also secured by a string belt. Unusual for Indians was the frequent wearing of the moustache among these tribes.

The most important part of dress was the blanket which wrapped the bodies of men, women and children. It was a beautiful piece of weaving in a mixture of cedar bark, mountain goat wool and dog's hair. Some blankets were fur-trimmed and an occasional, luxurious robe was fashioned of sea-otter skins. Sea-otter, almost extinct today, was found along the Pacific coast from Lower California to Alaska and in the eighteenth century was especially sought and prized by the Russians and the Chinese.

An inland group of Canadian Indians is the Caribou Eskimo, who were given that name by white men because from the caribou reindeer come the skins they wear, the sinews for thread, strings for snowshoes and nets, the meat they eat, and the bones and antlers which make their tools. The animal was hunted with bow and arrow but today hunting is done with gun and much of their food comes from the trader including tea which is brewed strong and black, a very popular drink.

In 1492 and 1493 Columbus came upon the scene, his two voyages commissioned by Ferdinand and Isabella with the new lands becoming realms of the Castilian crown. When he landed in the Bahamas he thought he had reached India, thus the names of Indians and West Indians. "Redskins," the newcomers called the aborigines, a misnomer because the natural coloring of their flesh ranged from brown to a lighter shade but the Indians painted themselves with a red pigment of vegetable and mineral extraction. So "Indians" and "Redskins" they became forever after.

When the news of Columbus' find reached England, she in 1497 and 1499 despatched expeditions under the command of the Venetian, Giovanni Gabotte (anglicized to John Cabot) to take possession of unknown lands for that kingdom. In touching at Labrador, he became the first white man to step upon the mainland. Norman and Breton fishermen are thought to have visited Newfoundland as early as 1500. In 1500, the Portuguese Commander Cabral, on a voyage to India with thirteen caravals from the Cape Verde Islands, landed in Brazil and took possession of Brazil claiming the discovery of the country. Americus Vespucci was an Italian navigator, cartographer and writer who took part in several trips to the New World. He wrote his memoirs, published in 1507, stressing his belief that the discovery was of a new world, and his geographer-publisher proposed America as the name for the southern continent. Over the years the use of the name spread, by the end of 1600 designating the northern continent as well.

Long before the white man's coming, there evolved many different Indian stocks, each with its own dialect as unrelated as European languages are to each other. The many cultures ranged from the most primitive to a truly complex organization. In southern pre-Columbian America the advanced state of culture suggests a time of many milleniums to have accomplished the rise. There existed three great civilizations, that of the Maya in Yucatan and Guatemala, the Incas in ancient Peru and the military empire of the Aztecs in Mexico. With centuries upon centuries behind them, a decadence had already set in when the Spanish conquistadors came, a fact which contributed to the success of the conquest.

The first sight of the Spaniards on their horses must have astounded the Indians, possibly leading them to think that the man on his handsome steed was a god. Forever after, the horse became a favored motif in weaving and drawing and all their artifacts.

The Maya civilization consisted of a group of races possessing an ancient culture which existed before the Christian Era. It rose to its height about 1000 A.D. Its people were advanced in art, architecture, engineering, astronomy, mathematics and a complex hieroglyphic form of writing but history, traditions and religious prophecies were passed on orally.

The Aztecs, originally a minor tribe, reached their height of culture in the thirteenth century but from then on a decline is to be noted. They founded the impregnable capital City of Mexico in 1325. When Cortéz arrived on the scene the Aztecs were the dominant race in Mexico. They had reached a high point in art, engineering, architecture, astronomy and mathematics. Drawing evolved into a pictographic writing. Their empire was destroyed by Cortéz and annexed to Spain in 1521.

The Inca civilization flourished during the early centuries of the Christian Era acquiring its greatest expansion from the fourteenth century on. The Incas had no writing as had the Maya and the Aztecs but in art, architecture, ceramics, mathematics, astronomy and gold work they were skilled to a high degree. Archaeological discoveries of our period have brought to light that the Incas were only a final phase in a long history of Peruvian cultures. The farmer developed and furnished to the world more than a dozen staple food-plants of our daily diet.

The working of copper, silver and gold by the Indians of these countries was a fine art. Basket weaving, and the spinning and weaving of cotton and the soft fleece of the llamas, were of such perfection both technically and artistically before the arrival of the invaders that many forms of the exquisite handwork done on simple stick looms remain unsurpassed today. The Peruvian women wore beautiful fabrics of yarns finer than is being produced by modern machinery. The Spaniards mistook the fine cotton and woolen cloth of the Indians' dress for silk. The use of sheep's wool came with the Spanish. Garments, the same as those worn hundreds of years ago, are still worn in the villages.

Because the weaving was done by hand on the narrow loom, costume design was of necessity straight and narrow. There were tunics long and short, fringed robes, crushed girdles, serapes or shawls and scarfs, all woven with colorful motifs, fine straw weaving and beautiful feather work. A short skirt and a sleeveless tunic was the feminine everyday dress; that of the man consisted of breechclout, hipcloth or wide sash and mantle. Elaborateness of costume distinguished the wearer, priests and officials being clothed in the most gorgeous robes enhanced further with ornaments of pure gold. Headdresses were wonderful creations invariably finished with the long quetzal plumes of

4

brilliant color. Footwear was of skins softly tanned and beautifully dyed in yellow, black and white. The explorer, De Soto, in his account expressly mentioned the vermilion leather as resembling broadcloth and the black as a "brilliant black."

The Incas used cotton, and fur which they called wool, in their weaving. They hunted the chinchilla for food and its luxurious coat. The small rodent got its name from an earlier civilized tribe, the Chincas whom the Incas conquered. The skins were made into mantles and there was a marvelous thistledown cloth of sheared "wool" of the little animal. The chinchilla was sheared periodically as sheep are shorn.

To the state belonged the great herds of llama which supplied wool for clothing, flesh for food and a form of tax payment. A constant spinning was carried on by the women of the upper class and the royal storehouses held large quantities of woolen garments for the army's use. The coarser wool of the llama was worn by the common people while the finer wool of the vicuña was reserved for the nobles. The king was always clothed anew for any state occasion, his wardrobe including a lavish mantle fashioned of brilliant birds' feathers, an art which these Indians perfected.

Quilted cotton was used by the Aztecs, in an overall garment resembling the modern union suit but very thick. Its thickness of three quarters to an inch proved such a real protection against javelins and arrows that the Spaniards adopted the armor. The Aztecs also carried small round shields which were impenetrable except at close range. Interwoven cane and cotton covered with painted boards was reinforced with feather work producing a shield which successfully warded off blows of the jagged blades of obsidian, a flint-like stone.

To the land of the North American Indians came a group of Huguenots in 1562 settling in Florida on Port Royal Sound and in 1564 on St. John's River where Fort Caroline was established. 1607 saw the founding of Jamestown Colony by the English in Virginia while 1620 marks the arrival of the Pilgrim Fathers on Cape Cod. 1626 is the date of the settlement of New Amsterdam by the Dutch and Peter Minuit's purchase of Manhattan Island from the Indians for the goodly sum of twenty-four dollars. The Swedes and Finns proclaimed a New Sweden in Delaware in 1638 and the Germans who became known as the "Pennsylvania Dutch" settled in that part of the country in 1683. And there we have the beginning of the world's great melting pot.

FIVE CENTURIES OF AMERICAN COSTUME

The term North American Indian covers many different stocks and even more diverse were the linguistic unlikenesses of which some two hundred and fifty languages and dialects are spoken today. They had a crude form of sign-writing but developed no real writing and therefore, no alphabet. All can be said to be of Asiatic stock with dark complexion, dark eyes and jet black hair. Hair on face and body was sparse and plucked if present but baldness of the head was unknown. As to the features, some have long faces, some have round faces, some have the aquiline nose while others have a broader, flatter nose. And some are tall, others short. Face painting with red pigment was part of war dress. A feminine note was the line of vermilion in the center parting of the hair, a brilliant touch that could be copied by any black-eyed beauty today.

Unlike the Indians of South America and Mexico and those along the Gulf of Mexico, the North American Indians wore few clothes of cloth. What covering was worn was usually of softly tanned animal skins. A general piece of male dress was the breechclout which consisted of two small leather aprons hanging from a narrow belt, one piece in front and one over the buttocks. Women wore a fringed skin tied round the waist in apron fashion, and young girls took to wearing a modesty piece when about thirteen years old. When indoors, neither man nor woman wore any covering above the waist, nor for that matter when outdoors in mild weather. Eventually the crusading priests who converted many of the Indians to the Christian faith, succeeded in getting the males into short breeches.

Indian boys in the East, who wore no shirt even in the coldest weather, did have arm muffs of fur which reached from wrist to shoulder, were laced up the sides and secured by thongs around the neck. A soft beaver robe thrown over the left shoulder and belted at the waist protected the bare body against the rigors of winter.

Tattooing was a favorite form of ornamentation on body and face, some chiefs elaborately tattooed from head to toe. Women were tattooed too, but in more delicate design, usually arms and legs in bracelet fashion. Over the years the practice waned in the east as the Indian became accustomed to the white man's dress which covered his body. Tattooing was still practiced in the west in the 1830's when George Catlin, the artist-author, painted among the western tribes. He noted that both the masculine and feminine bodies were so decorated, the design applied by pricking vermilion and gunpowder into the skin.

The outdoor garment was the robe or blanket of grass or hemp for cool weather and the animal skin which wrapped round and over the head for winter use. The pelts of all available animals were put to use, moose, deer, beaver, otter, opossum, raccoon, wolf, badger, fox, squirrel and in the west, bison which was wrongly called buffalo by the Europeans. A deerskin robe with the tail and paws attached was a treasure. Robes intended for summer wear were usually finished without the hair. The winter robe was left furred to be worn fur inside and also to serve as a sleeping cover.

The European found that the Indian had perfected his method of tanning using the brains of the animal to oil-tan deer and buckskin to the texture of the finest chamois, a secret they passed on to the colonist. A contemporary note states that moose skins were made "wondrous white." On a par with the status of the mink coat in today's feminine wardrobe was the mantle of wild turkey feathers, the brilliant, iridescent plumes applied to a woven cloth of grass twine and so well done that the foundation was completely concealed by the feathers.

According to letters and drawings of the explorers it would seem that the Indians from Virginia and along the Pacific coast from Mexico to Alaska generally went barefoot. Grass or fiber sandals covered the feet of the Mexican natives, the southwest desert country and South America while the northerners of the upper Mississippi and New England locales wore moccasins and leggings. The man's leggings reached to the thigh, secured by being tied to the belt of the breechclout. The woman's leggings reached only to the knees, held by a string garter.

The moccasin resembled the primitive European shoe, the carbatine, being fashioned of a single piece of leather for the foot but differing in a flap round the ankle. The Indian of the forest wore a soft-soled shoe, his plainsman brother fortifying the sole with heavier leather. The flaps of footwear and the seams of robes and pouches were finished with embroidery of tiny beads made from shells, cut-up quills of birds and porcupine, moose bristles, pearls and sometimes copper. Later, the Indian who was always eager for new ideas in dress made use of European beads.

The headband was the common form of headdress, principally to keep the hair off the face. Of skin dyed black, or red bietta cloth which the wearer procured by barter with the whites, it was decorated with beadwork and held a row of upstanding quill feathers. The eagle and turkey feathers of the forest

Indians stood upright, the feathers of the plains Indians drooping backward. Every bit as smart as the modish pillbox of the modern lady was a cap worn in the north along the Canadian border, a real pillbox shape which the French called a "capote," trimmed with tiny shells, beads and perhaps a few feathers spreading from the center of the crown.

Indians groomed their heads, there being a variance of style according to tribe and location. As a rule the Indians of the east from Georgia to Lake Champlain shaved and cropped the head leaving a ridge of hair from center top to the nape. This was the roach or crest and we find the Indians of New York and New England often fashioned an artificial roach of deer's tail bristles, a more luxurious ornament than the natural one. Those that grew long hair dressed it with oil and bear's grease. The Florida Indians rolled the hair to a topknot. Some of the Plains chiefs in the nineteenth century often grew very long hair, long enough to touch the ground. Worn flowing, it was especially effective when riding horseback. Indians of the Great Lakes and the upper Mississippi region braided their long hair.

The early war bonnet was the headdress of the western and Canadian Indians when off to war but, since the nineteenth century, was also adopted by the eastern Indians who wear it upon festive occasions. Each feather represented a special deed or "coup" performed, and had to be plucked from the golden eagle by the chief himself. He also had to capture the bird and release it unharmed after taking the quills because the eagle was revered as the king of birds. Some modern western tribes raise semi-trained eagles for the feathers. In the more usual headdress of one, two or three quills, the plumes were notched to record each "coup."

Women prided themselves on the beauty of their hair, wearing it flowing, braided or clubbed with the front cut in a fringe. Most unusual and handsome is the contemporary headdress of the Seminole matron dating from the late nineteenth century and the pompadour of the Gibson Girl Era. She combs her long hair over her head tying it at the forehead, then spreading it over a frame like a poke-bonnet brim and tucking it underneath. A net holds the hair in place and the result is a flattering hairdo and hat combination as shown on page 27.

The costume of the Florida Seminoles, a tribe which developed after the American Revolution, is unique. These Indians were a split-off of the Creek

Nation which originally occupied Georgia, Alabama and northern Florida. During the 1830's, in resistance to being removed to a reservation in Oklahoma, they hid out in the Everglades of Florida where the United States troops were unsuccessful in following the "Runaways" or Seminoles, both words meaning the same thing. Here, many escaped African slaves from Georgia and Alabama joined them. At first the negroes were slaves to the Indians but eventually intermarriage took place so that today, many Seminoles are of mixed blood.

The contemporary feminine costume of these Indians is a colorful and graceful dress of European influence. A long, full skirt is topped by a deep, flaring ruffle falling from a yoke to the hips creating a beautiful line for almost any figure since the skirt covers the feet. Not a gown one would expect in a swampland! With it is worn the combination hat-headdress. Remarkable is the fabric made possible by the invention of the sewing machine, of which every woman owns a portable hand-turning model. Narrow rows and rows of brightly colored cotton cloth are machine-stitched together horizontally forming a kaleidoscopic pattern for a skirt yards around, and for the deep bertha. In men's dress, formerly the breechclout or a pair of skin breeches sufficed, but today, if not attired in the "long shirt" of the same gay material, he may be seen in factory-made cotton shirt and slacks. Dresses for little boys and girls are also fashioned of the decorative cottons.

Jewelry has always been part of Indian dress in copper and silver, particularly bracelets, necklaces and earrings. The earrings were suspended from holes pierced round the outer edge of the ear. Indians of standing, principally the chiefs, liked breast plates of silver, shell and other materials. They were especially eager to own silver gorgets such as the European officers wore and considered it a signal honor to receive one from a white man.

The pouch was an important accessory in Indian dress and usually swung from the string belt holding his fire-making tools, his pipe and tobacco. The eastern Indian copied the white man's bandolier with pockets, such appurtenances made showy with quill and beadwork.

The Indian woman had a carry-all, a wonderful convenience, the value of which is just being recognized by some modern young mothers. It is the baby frame, centuries old: a clever, practical piece making it easy to carry the baby on one's back, set it down on bench, or the back seat of the car, or even hang it on a nail. And so simple: three pieces compose the contraption: the board, the foot board and the bow or arch over which the headcloth drapes. See page 27.

Slowly, over the centuries the Indian has taken on those parts of the white man's dress that fit into his way of living. Factory-made clothes are replacing much of the picturesque costume. But on the whole, after some four and half centuries of contact with European stock, the Indian remains distinctly himself, an individual and the first American.

Norsemen
9th and 10th Centuries

helmet, sword and axe of iron·wooden shield covered with hide and reinforced with iron·belt and straps of hide· fur corselet· cross·gartered leggings· hide carbatines· woolen mantle

helmet, javelin and sword of iron·jazeran (scaled corselet) of linen or hide with metal scales· belt, straps and carbatines(shoes) of hide·cross· gartered trousers· woolen mantle· sheath gilded and engraved

helmet, sword and axe of iron· woolen tunic with embroidery·belt, straps and sandals of hide·cross· gartered trousers· fur mantle

casque (spangenhelm) of pieced iron·javelin, sword and axe of iron· wooden·shield covered with hide reinforced with iron· jazeran of linen or hide with metal scales·belt, and straps of hide· cross·gartered trousers· carbatines of hide

RTW

Eskimos

parkeh of seal or
reindeer skin with fur inside-
bearskin trousers-
mukleks of unhaired
seal or walrus-
wolverine collar
with bead
fringe-
Alaskan
Eskimo
woman

parkeh of seal-
fur side in-
fringed with
dog fur-
mukleks of
walrus hide-
painted
leather trim-
Canadian
caribou
Eskimo

sealskin parkeh with
painted leather trim-
sealskin mukleks
(hip boots)- fur
side in-
wolverine hood-
Alaskan
Eskimo

ensemble of caribou skin-
parkeh, trousers, boots and gloves-
tunic edged with
red leather
leather fringe-
Canadian
caribou
Eskimo

RTW

Eskimos-modern

parkeh of brown and white
caribou skin-white
leather fringe-
hood of wolverine
or bear fur-
sealskin bands-
zippered boots-
pouch belt and
trim of colored
leather-
Canadian
caribou
Eskimo

calico dress over
fur parkeh-fox or
wolverine hood-
deerskin boots
over sealskin
socks and
woolen
stockings-
fur-lined
mittens-
young
Eskimo girl

printed cotton dress over fur parkeh-
fur-lined hood for carrying baby-
little tot in calico over fur parkeh-
fur hood- deerskin breeches-
fur side in-
Alaskan
Eskimos-
Bering
Beach

navy blue cotton dress
over fur parkeh-blue
underslip- deerskin or
wolverine hood-
zippered
leather boots in
gray and white-
Alaskan
Eskimo

RTW

skirt formed of long scarf embroidered and jade-fringed-knotted scarf of contrasting color-headdress of gold, jewels and tiny feathers-swirl of own hair-chieftain's daughter

embroidered robe and sash-tied cloth headband-gold ornaments and feathers-hair bound with ribbon-nobleman going to ceremonial

priest dressed in jaguar skin-gold ornaments, jade and turqoise-quetzal plumage

mother in wrapped skirt-baby in "rebozo"-handloomed silky-looking cotton or woolen scarfs-farmer's wife-ancient and modern

RTW

Aztec

fan signifies
a diplomat-
colorful
embroidered
robe-gold and
jade jewelry-
headdress of
gold ornaments
and quetzal
plumage

young girl in
fringed and
embroidered
tunic and wrapped,
scarf skirt-
tied headband

young girl in
tunic embroidered
and appliqued-
wrapped, fringed
scarf skirt-
tied headband

warrior on way
to ceremonial-
quilted tunic
with painted
tabs-jeweled
leg-bands-
tied headband
with panache
of feathers,
gold, turquoise
and jade

RTW

government official
in striped cotton
robe-tall hat with
embroidery, gold
and jewels

farmer wearing
long loin scarf
with embroidered
motifs-painted
leather helmet-
gourd for
carrying water

dress of cotton in
brilliant deep color-
cotton motifs
embroidered and
appliquéd with
contrasting
tones

white cotton frocks
with multicolored
embroidery-
children of
an official

RTW

reminiscent of Andalusian
dress - red velvet bodice
with lace frill
and embroidery -
green velvet skirt -
dark gray
felt chola (hat) -
silk stockings
with sandals

bright red
woolen
poncho - striped
black and
white - black
knee breeches -
montera of black
felt with white
cord trim -
farmer

woolen poncho,
red, gray and black -
black woolen
trousers - chullo, a
stockingette cap-
red with white
design - commonly
worn under
the montera
(see above)

all cloth costume - hat,
shoulder mantle and jacket
in red - purple skirts - green
apron - trim
in red, green,
black and white -
woman's montera
(hat) edged
with notched
green cloth -
sandals and
silk stockings

FTW

Indians of Florida
16th Century

witch doctor-
hair cropped to a
roach-bluebird
attached-animal
skin apron-
bladder pouch
with leather
fringe

chief-
tattooed body-
leather belt
and pouch-
ornaments of
copper-hair
dressed up in
topknot-feather
and raccoon
tail

young woman
wearing a scarf
of palm fronds

Virginia chief-
fringed deerskin
apron with tail-
hair cropped
to a roach-
tied knot in
back-small
feathers

RTW

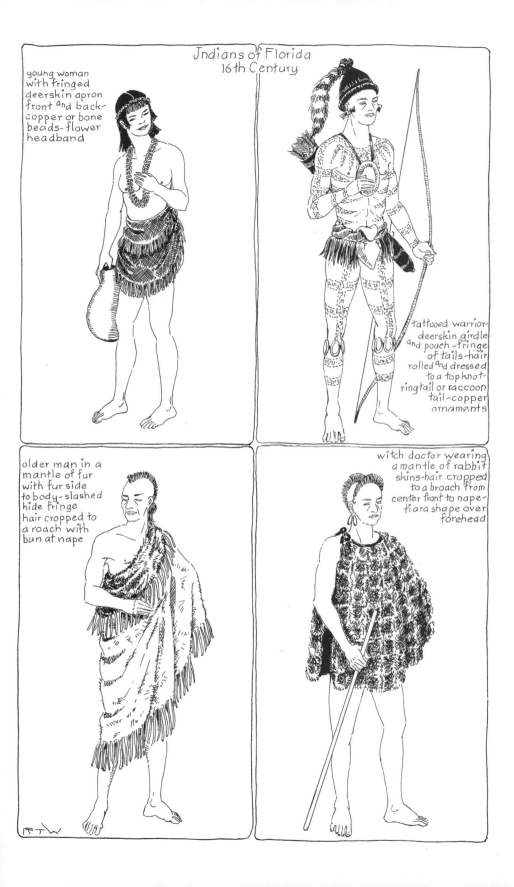

Indians of Florida
16th Century

young woman
with fringed
deerskin apron
front and back-
copper or bone
beads-flower
headband

tattooed warrior-
deerskin girdle
and pouch-fringe
of tails-hair
rolled and dressed
to a top knot-
ringtail or raccoon
tail-copper
ornaments

older man in a
mantle of fur
with fur side
to body-slashed
hide fringe
hair cropped to
a roach with
bun at nape

witch doctor wearing
a mantle of rabbit
skins-hair cropped
to a broach from
center front to nape-
tiara shape over
forehead

Indians of the 17th Century

Eastern Indian with wild turkey-frilled white linen European shirt-deerskin leggings-fringed side seams and red trim-fastened to beaded belt-skin pouches in belt-feathers fastened to roach

Algonquian chief of Rhode Island-cloth breechclout-fur mantle-bead headband and belt-silver disks, chain and turquoise beads-deerskin boots-1637

Indians of New Sweden on the Delaware-mother and daughter-evidence of Swedish influence in silver ornaments and woven pieces-cloth cap and kilt-painted water gourd-"the long horn"

Algonquian chief, King Philip-c.1675-European white linen, collared shirt-beaded pillbox hat, necklace and belt-powder horn-cloth mantle-deerskin boots

Iroquois dress-Colonial Period in dyed deerskin with white porcupine quill embroidery-changed later to European fabrics in broadcloth, cottons and beads-never changed style or color-belt, sash and crossed bands, red with white-red leggings with blue and white, tied at knees-green kilt with white-turban red, green and white with eagle feathers-silver disk on chain

Iroquois dress-Colonial Period in dyed deerskin with porcupine quill embroidery-later, changed to European fabrics in broadcloth, cottons and beads-never changed style or color-red overdress with blue and white embroidery-white cotton frills-dark blue skirt with white embroidery-pantalets tied at knees-red with blue and white embroidery-woolen mantle-moccasins

Red Jacket-1758?-1830-Seneca chief and orator-red jacket presumably that presented to him by a British officer-braid and bead fringe trim-red silk sash-white linen shirt and cravat-silver medal, gift of Washington-deerskin leggings and moccasins-fur cap-based on portrait by R. W. Weir

one of the chiefs who visited London-therefore, buckled shoes with "red heels" signifying royal birth-velvet coat-satin breeches-silk stockings-velvet cap-beaded belt-woolen mantle-1710

RTW

Indians
18th Century

Iroquois warrior-
fur, tail-edged
blanket-headdress
of wheat spikes-earrings
of polished stones-red
leaf ornament-green
deerskin leggings-
leather boots, natural
color-pouch-pipe
tomahawk-simple
tomahawk-war club-
1780's

red woolen mantle with
blue border and scalp locks-
deerskin skirt
with scalp locks-
beaded belt with
small dead
animal-beaded
deerskin leggings
and moccasins-
toque of birds'
breasts and
feathers-two
eagle plumes-
silver medal-
Seneca
chief-
1790's

colored woolen mantle-white linen shirt-
silver armlets-chain with locket-beaded
cord holding smoking
pipe and tobacco
pouch-leather
baldric-black
leather leggings-
deerskin moccasins-
rifle-Mohawk chief-
1780's

Creek Indian who visited London-
padded silk mantle
with ribbon bands-
white linen shirt-
silver armlets-
silver gorget-
jeweled necklace-
a feathery nosegay
headdress-tattoo
on forehead-
black leather
leggings-
deerskin
moccasins-
1760's

RTW

deerskin tunic and
leggings-tunic
natural color-
leggings golden
yellow-brilliant
porcupine quill work-
fringe of thinned out
scalp locks-
pipe of
steatite wound
with braid of
porcupine
quill work-
black
moccasins-
chief

painted red
stripes on torso-
pink-dyed
leggings-red
stripe-blue sash-
apron front and
back-buffalo
robe, collar and
collarette-
porcupine quill
embroidery-
bead necklace-
bow and
arrows-
"mystery drum-
witch doctor

buffalo hide overdress-porcupine quill
embroidery-
sleeves fringed
with scalp

locks-deerskin
leggings-
headdress of
ermine skins,
buffalo
horns,

variegated
colored
ribbons
and
feathers-
"medicine
bag," an
animal
skin
stuffed
with moss
or grass-
witch
doctor

mother in dress of mountain goatskin
with porcupine embroidery-
fringe of scalp locks-
boy in dyed deerskin
leggings and moccasins
and apron

RTW

Crow Indians famed for long hair sometimes reaching to the ground-painted mantle of buffalo skin-headdress of eagle quills, small feathers and colored stones-necklace and earrings of same-deerskin leggings and moccasins-1830's

Ottoe Indian in coat of grizzly bear pelt and claws-deerskin leggings and moccasins-bead embroidery and ribbon fringe-headdress of eagle quills mounted on red cap with shells, silver band and ornaments-silver medal-pipe with scalp locks-1830's

Osage brave with ruff of feathers-deerskin apron, leggings and moccasins with bead and wampum embroidery-blue silk breech cloth-rose silk garters with scalp locks-silver bracelets-bow and arrows-1830's

Choctaw Indian in ball-playing dress-body tattooed or painted-breech cloth and beaded belt-mane of dyed horsehair round neck-tail of white or dyed horsehair and quills-1830's

RTW

Mandan chief - tunic of
mountain sheep skin-quill
embroidery - scalp
locks on skirt-
bonnet and trim of
ermine and
ermine tails, horns
war eagle feathers-
deerskin leggings
with self fringe
at side seams-
feathers and
scalp locks
tied to
lance-
1830's

chief of Sacs and Foxes-
shirt and leggings of
mountain goat skin-
headdress, red
plumage and eagle
quill-multicolored
silk sash-red
breech cloth-
red flaps at
knees and
moccasins-
red woolen
blanket, blue
border-

buffalo claw
necklace-
silver armlets-
tomahawk-
leather shield
with tails-
lance with
feathers-
1830's

favorite wife of the above chief of
the Sacs and Foxes-costume
of "civilized stuffs" in multi-pastel-
colors-bodice, pantalets
and band on skirt, red-
shawl over shoulders
covered with pinned-on
silver brooches-
1830½

Crow chief in
tunic of mountain
goat skin-leggings
of deerskin-
quill embroidery
fringed with
scalp locks-
headdress of
war eagle quills
and ermine tails-
shield and
quiver of
buffalo hide-
lance with eagle
quills and scalp
locks-1830's

RTW

Seminole Indians
19th and 20th Centuries

Seminole Chief Osceola-costume of printed cotton cloth-turban of cotton shawl with ostrich plumes-bead belt with silver disks and scalp locks-beads and silver gorgets-silver bracelets with scalp locks-red buckskin leggings with

blue tops and scalp locks-yellow moccasins and above knees-rifle, powder horn, and sheepskin pouch-1830's

tunic of silk with rose and white design on blue ground-tan cotton fringed skirt with green and yellow border-yellow bertha with rose and red trim-beads and silver ornaments-ribbon headdress-1830's

contemporary Seminole dress-variegated colored strips of cotton cloth sewn together-made possible by the sewing machine-hair dressed over frame-influence of pompadour fashion 1890's-hair worn flowing by young women

contemporary Seminole dress-"the long shirt"-also worn with slacks-made by the women of variegated colored stripes of cotton cloth sewn together on a portable sewing machine-turban band of same

RTW

Indian

Zuni woman of Pueblo land - hand-woven, black dress which has not changed since pre-Columbian days - beaded belt - silver and turquoise jewelry new in 19th C.

white deerskin leggings and boots

the roach headdress - head shaved or cropped - artificial roach of deer hair worn by New York and New England Indians

chief's headdress of eagle feathers - New England Indian - 17th C.

baby frame of wood - beaded and embroidered red and blue cloth

Guatemalan headdress - "tzute" - hand-woven cloth - 30 by 40 inches - folded, used as basket pad, as protection against sun or as a carry-all

"squash blossom" coiffure - traditional headdress for young Hopi women - 1893

Pueblo Indian dancer - black dress - beaded red belt - red, black and white shawl - white deerskin leggings and moccasins - silver jewelry

Seminole coiffure and hat in one - fashioned of the wearer's hair - drawn up from the neck to the forehead - tied and spread over a cardboard frame on top - then drawn under and tucked in - secured by a net

chief's crown of eagle feathers and ermine tails - New England Indian - 17th C.

an ingenious turban - a length of red felt about two inches wide wound round a wadded roll and twisted into shape on the head - Contemporary Guatemalan

RTW

MILITARY
1492 TO 1700

CHAPTER TWO

TRAINED ARMIES OF SOLDIERS date back to ancient times. The Egyptians, Babylonians, Assyrians, Persians, Greeks and Romans each in turn had powerful warrior troops in uniform. Then came the so-called "Dark Ages" when wars continued to be fought but the fighters carried on their warfare in motley or everyday clothes.

The modern uniform of armed bodies of men had its beginning in the late Medieval Period when the retainers who lived and worked on the lands of the feudal lords followed their masters into battle. These retainers wore the colors and insignia of their knight, but there were also mercenaries of other countries who were hired and paid to fight. They wore clothing of their own choice in fabric and color and according to their means. Gradually ensigns, flags and standards came to designate the opposing sides of battle and became a mark of home base to the fighter.

In the fourteenth century, the Swiss soldiers, who were the first to adopt an insignia, wore badges, sprigs of oak or pine, straw, corn, a colored feather in the helmet, or a cross of white linen sewn to the tunic. In another instance of the Swiss distinguishing marks, a black bear was painted on the iron-plate armor. This eventually led to silk scarfs of a certain color being wound round the waist or neck and, in turn, to enforcement of some rules pertaining to the soldiers' dress.

At the time of the discoveries in the New World, the soldiers of the European nations were still clothed in the armorial colors furnished by the prince or sovereign who employed them. To America came soldiers from various countries, Spain, Portugal, France, the Low Countries, England, Sweden and Germany. The favorite color for "liveries," as such clothing was termed, was red, the retainer receiving two suits a year from his commander.

This was the period of armor which was worn over regular dress or a fitted suit of thick cloth or leather much like the modern union suit. Armor was not new, having been worn by the Egyptians, Greeks and Romans. The beautiful Gothic armor of the fifteenth century was built with fluted surfaces and edges to deflect the thrust of sword and lance. Armor reached its perfection and its most artistic stage at the turn of the sixteenth century but it became too heavy and, at the same time, the improvement of firearms lessened its usefulness. Foot soldiers were not provided with armor, wearing either a padded jacket or a chain hauberk. This century marked the decline of armor, owing to the progress made in artillery.

Crossbow and arrow disappeared after the Battle of Paris in 1525 and new bodies of troops were formed of gunners, pikemen, light horsemen and cavalrymen. The gunners no longer wore armplates while the lancers wore only breastplate and shoulder pieces. Light horse cavalry wore almost complete armor while German cavalrymen wore no cuirass but a doublet of buffskin and a felt hat with turned-up brim and boots. Officers discarded the helmet, wearing instead the slouch felt hat decorated with a panache. And foot soldiers wore a casque-shaped helmet with neck cover and ear flaps.

Armor as part of British Army dress disappeared in the last decade of the seventeenth century. The breastplate, worn but occasionally, was especially liked by painter and sitter as an artistic piece of still life in a portrait. The cuirass survived for a while in a shaped yoke of steel to protect neck and shoulders. When no longer a protection, it became the ornamental gorget, a small crescent of steel or silver plate suspended from a chain round the neck as insignia of an officer's rank in full dress. British officers stationed in the American Colonies sometimes bestowed the gorget upon an Indian chief in recognition of service, a reward that was highly appreciated by the recipient.

Though in many countries, large units of fighting men composed of civilians and rustics still wore their ordinary working clothes in service, it was first in France that the wearing of uniform dress began to be governed by rule. Occasionally, a wealthy colonel put his men into uniform at his own expense, the uniform, however, remaining his property. A colonel was responsible to his commander-in-chief for the welfare of his regiment, in charge not only of its clothing but responsible also for the condition of the armament. Cavalry and infantry too, came under this arrangement in which the colonel of the regiment chose the color, cloth and style of the uniforms.

Spain, the leading military power of the sixteenth century, became a strong influence in western fashions and etiquette, a lead she held into the seventeeth century. Army dress now followed the elegant Spanish bombasted silhouette as did the rest of Europe. The peasecod-bellied doublet with short skirt and puffed trunk hose became high fashion both in civilian and military life. The long, silk, knitted hose were protected by a shorter pair called boot hose. The lobster-tailed steel helmet, cuirass and gorget survived the century but, as the use of heavy armor declined, the leather jerkin or buffcoat took its place. The doublet, or padded, fitted underbody called a waistcoat, took to civilian wear as the corset for men, women and children, to be worn for centuries to come.

A fantastic military dress was that of the Lansquenets, German-Swiss mercenaries of the fifteenth and sixteenth centuries. They were foot soldiers carrying crossbow, lance and the heavy, two-handed sword, who delighted in fancy dress of velvet, satin, brocades and embroideries or whatever was available. The Germans copied the Swiss soldiers who, when they won the battle against the Duke of Burgundy, mended their ragged clothes with strips of tents, banners and furnishings left behind by the fleeing Burgundians. High-crowned felt hats were ornamented with scarfs and sweeping plumes.

From 1618 to 1648 the greater part of the European continent was engaged in the Thirty Years War in which men were almost constantly at battle. Military dress, what there was of it, followed the mode of the day in civilian clothes, the only difference being in heavier cloth for body protection. So long a siege of military activity was bound to bring about a change, one in which the mercenary troops were retained and converted into standing armies, each power now giving consideration to the establishment of a permanent force. In 1635 the French cavalry squadrons were organized into regiments.

The seventeenth century saw the decline of the Spanish corseted mode and the Paris of Louis XIII (1601–1643) taking over as arbiter of European court dress. This was the chevalier or cavalier fashion which brings to mind the aristocratic portraits of the great Flemish painter, Sir Anthony Van Dyck (1599–1641), an age often noted as the Van Dyck Period. It is also known as the age of "The Three Musketeers," that ever-thrilling tale written by Alexander Dumas. Soldiers wearing these costumes came to our shores. Out of this fashion, which really originated in the Low Countries, evolved the soldier's buffcoat of buffalo hide, a very comfortable and important garment. The buffcoat of chamoised leather, a costly piece of apparel, was worn at first either under or over the cuirass, but by mid-century officers wore it with longer and flaring skirt edged with fur, the skirt slashed into four panels, the better for horseback.

From here on our interest centers on the British soldiers and the German mercenaries in service with them in the American Colonies. The Georges of England were kings of Great Britain and Hanover. Thus it was that Hanoverian regiments, especially those from Hesse-Cassel and Hesse-Darmstadt, were frequently brigaded with British troops on the continent and in the colonies. Many of these Hessians remained after the war to make America their home.

The British were the earliest of the European powers in the actual development of an army uniform. The first standing army in England was established in 1645 when Parliament under Oliver Cromwell raised its own army for permanent service. France, despite her reputation in the military field, did not get into line in army dress until later in the century.

As time wore on the coat of scarlet cloth became the mark of the British soldier, by the end of the century differing only in the color of the regimental facings of the various units. Breeches were gray, white, blue, yellow or any color the wearer desired, in fact the scarlet coat was the only uniform part of the dress. Occasionally, a commander when in mourning for a member of his family put his men into mourning with black facings on the scarlet coat. It was at the funeral of Cromwell in 1658 that the London Foot Soldiers were furnished with such coats by the Lord Protector's son. Another like instance was that of Lord Chesterfield whose men were attired in red coats lined with black and carried black flags with red crosses.

A long waistcoat of buff leather worn under the scarlet coat was the dress of the light horse troops in 1661 and eventually, the uniform of all British cavalry regiments and finally, of almost all the line infantry everywhere in Europe up to the advent of the shako and coatee of the eighteenth century.

The complete costume comprised coat, waistcoat, breeches, black stockings reaching above the knees and gaiters over shoes or boots. Officers' dress was of the same pattern as that of the men but in fabric of superior quality ornamented with gold and silver braid and embroidery. An officer also wore a luxurious silk sash in the national colors and sword and gorget.

In headgear the morion and the lobster-tailed helmets lasted into the mid-

31

century. A gray, broad-brimmed hat of beaver felt which the English called the "slouch," enhanced with braid and plumage, often accompanied the uniform even when in action, in which case an iron skullcap was worn underneath. The "scull" when not in use was carried in the saddle bows.

The floppy hat evolved into the cocked hat. At first the brim was looped up to one side for convenience, then looped to the other side making it a three-cornered hat. Next, it was cocked front and back into the so-called Khevenhuller, Androsmane or Swiss style. Another military hat was the Monmouth cock, named after the Duke of Monmouth (1649–1685), son of Charles II. When companies of Grenadiers were added to the infantry in the latter part of 1600, the wide-brimmed hat was found inconvenient in throwing hand grenades so that in the British Army a fur-banded cap with tasseled bag was substituted. Named the grenadier cap, the frontal rose high like a shield, in metal or embroidered cloth, the tail grew small and disappeared, shaping finally into the tall fur cap of the grenadiers and fusiliers of the eighteenth century.

The wearing of wigs did not become general in England till the Restoration in 1660 when Charles II returned from his exile spent at the court of Louis XIV, wearing a black, full-bottomed wig. Periwig, it became in English, a contraction of the French perruque, the word assuming such contortions as peruyke, perewyke, periwig, winding up finally as just plain "wig." Soldier, sportsman and traveler adopted the short, bob wig and the short campaign wig, this latter dressed in two curls which hung down in back over each shoulder. Soldiers also plaited their natural hair and tucked it up in back under the cap. Occasionally, when long hair was required in military dress, flowing horsehair hung in back attached to the edge of the cap.

Officers, however, wore the large, heavy, curled, greased and powdered wig with large cocked and plumed hat, truly an absurd getup when in action. In the ranks, about 1684, the hair was bobbed or else tied back for convenience and then, the silk bag appeared some time before 1700, worn first by the army. This style, considered négligé and disrespectful, soon won the approval of the élite in civil life for the very special reason that it protected collar and coat from a layer of powder. Powder applied over a base of candle grease or pomade was at first used in grayish white, light brown or tan, pure white not appearing until 1703.

This was the period of the boot, of velvets and fine soft leather in civil life but soldiers and real horsemen wore the heavy jack boot which was made bulkier-looking by spurs and broad spur leathers. It was called the kettle boot but more popular was the name "jack boot" because made of jack leather, a waxed leather coated with tar or pitch, the same as that employed for the blackjack, a huge jug or tankard which held ale or beer. Heels attached to shoes and boots came in about 1600, a feature which flattered masculine vanity in adding height to one's stature. Eagerly adopted by both sexes, we have had heels ever since. Also to be noted were the leggings and gaiters worn from the end of the century on.

The use of jack leather brings us to seamen's garb of short, full breeches, a tunic, a short jacket and a bonnet. Jacked leather originated in England, appearing first in the fourteenth century, whence the colloquialism by which the sailor is known in the English-speaking world as "Jack-tar" because of his tarred leather jacket and bonnet. The practical outfit spread over Europe and has been worn with some variations by Dutchmen, Germans, Italians and Frenchmen for some four centuries. The original design was that of the Basque seaman of the Mediterranean Sea, the loose breeches and tunic permitting acrobatic movement aboard the sailing ship. Of the sixteenth century was the truncated hat of fur or leather.

The uniform of the marine or sea soldier finally settled into a bloused shirt of canvas or coarse linen with open, lay-down collar over which went a doublet or waistcoat of homespun buttoned down center front. And over that the short, heavy, padded cloth or leather jacket which today is called a pea jacket. The full breeches were secured by a sturdy leather belt which also held pouch, knife and pistol. The loosely knotted neckerchief also served as headkerchief and a knitted woolen cap was a favorite.

Here in America the Dutch port of New Amsterdam became one of the most cosmopolitan cities in this hemisphere. Settled in 1626 by the Dutch West Indian Company, it was granted a monopoly of trade in Africa and America. The city grew into a base for the trading of furs and slaves as well, there being no stigma attached to the latter enterprise in those days. Visiting soldiers and sailors roamed the streets of the busy Atlantic seaport with sailing ships from world ports docked at its wharves.

Spanish
16th Century

engraved
steel
cuirass-
linen shirt
with lace-
paned trunk
hose-wrinkled
taffeta canions-
knit woolen
stockings-leather
boots-morion
with ear flaps-
dagger-pole-arm
1564

peasecod-bellied
boublet with trunk
hose and canions-
silk, paned and
slashed-lawn
collar and
cuffs with
lace-baldric
of gold chains-
clocked silk
stockings-
leather shoes-
silk toque with
jeweled band
and feathers-
military
commander-
1564

striped velvet and silk
peasecod
doublet-military
sash-trunk hose-
canions-silk toque
with feathers-neck
and sleeve ruffs-musket
and forked rest, sword
and tasseled powder
flask-military
commander-
1581

black armor with
white Malta cross-
"combed" morion-
green sash-green
velvet full slops-
white stockings-
yellow shoes-
military
commander-
1570's

RTW

French
16th Century

felt
hat-
slashed
doublet
and slashed
Spanish slops
with cuffs-
neck and
sleeve frills-
tailored
cloth stockings-
leather shoes-
dagger
and pole-arm-
1563

doublet
and Venetians-
buttons and
braid-lawn
collar and cuffs-
knit stockings-
leather shoes-
felt hat with
ribbon and
feathers-

musket and
forked rest-
bandoleer with
tubes of powder-
sword
1585

doublet and Venetians-
braid trim-lawn
collar and cuffs-silk
sash-felt hat with
jewel and feathers-knit
stockings-leather shoes-
pole-arm and sword
captain of
honor guard-
1596

typical sailor's garb-middle Europe-
tunic of jacked leather-
pantaloons of
heavy, coarse
canvas or woolen
cloth-bonnet
of goat or
lambskin-
leather shoes-1568

RTW

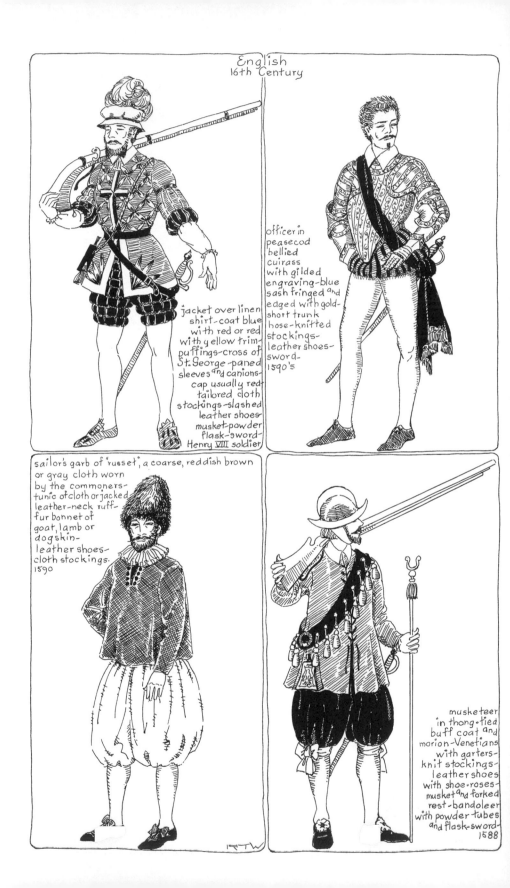

English
16th Century

jacket over linen
shirt-coat blue
with red or red
with yellow trim-
puffings-cross of
St. George-paned
sleeves and canions-
cap usually red-
tailored cloth
stockings-slashed
leather shoes-
musket-powder
flask-sword-
Henry VIII soldier

officer in
peasecod
bellied
cuirass
with gilded
engraving-blue
sash fringed and
edged with gold-
short trunk
hose-knitted
stockings-
leather shoes-
sword-
1590's

sailor's garb of "russet", a coarse, reddish brown
or gray cloth worn
by the commoners-
tunic of cloth or jacked
leather-neck ruff-
fur bonnet of
goat, lamb or
dogskin-
leather shoes-
cloth stockings.
1590

musketeer
in thong-tied
buff coat and
morion-Venetians
with garters-
knit stockings-
leather shoes
with shoe-roses-
musket and forked
rest-bandoleer
with powder-tubes
and flask-sword-
1588

16th Century

foot soldier-paned and slashed costume of cloth and silk-tailored cloth hose with codpiece-leather shoes-felt hat with plumes-Swiss and German mercenaries-Lansquenets-1st half of century

paned and slashed costume of cloth and silk-girdle of silk puffs-ruffs at neck and wrists-felt hat with plumes-knit stockings-leather shoes-Flemish-1580's

costume of slashed cloth-Venetians and doublet over linen shirt-silk sash-knit hose-bonnet of jacked leather with silk band-tasseled powder flask and musket-tasseled sabretache-Dutch-1580's

braided cloth winged doublet-silk scarf-shirt with rosettes-"Spanish Slops" with cloth panes and garters-codpiece fastened with rosettes-felt hat with plumes-leather shoes-cloth hose-pole-arm, dagger and sword-Swiss 1584

RTW

16th Century

marine officer in cloth doublet over collared shirt - braided pantaloons - bonnet of jacked leather, ribbon band and pompon - leather shoes - two-handed sword - dagger - Dutch - 1581

cuirass and gorget with ruff - embossed chain decoration - paned trunk hose and codpiece - sword and dagger belts passed under ribbon panes - knit tights or hose - leather shoes - Austrian - 1570

lansquenet with two-handed sword - 8 to 10 feet long - cuirass and cuisses - cabasset with plumes - slashed Venetians - leather boots -

foot soldier - Swiss and German

sailor carrying oar - suit of heavy canvas - braid trim - breast and pantaloon pockets - neck and wrist ruffs - leather shoes - bonnet of jacked leather - tobacco pipe on cord - Dutch - 1581

RTW

buffcoat winged and braided worn over uniform jacket-white linen falling band-breeches with gold braid and garters-knit hose-leather shoes-ribbon garters-beaver hat with braid and plumes-Dutch soldier-1608

sleeveless buffcoat worn over winged uniform jacket-embroidered linen falling band and cuffs-knit hose-leather boots with spurs-beaver hat with plumes-bandoleer with powder flasks-musket-forked rest-sword-English musketeer-1620

blue cassock with gold braid and buttons-linen shirt with falling band and puffed sleeves-baldric embroidered and fringed-red breeches, garters and stockings-black beaver hat with white ostrich fringe-red and white plumes-British officer-1660

musketeer in madder red uniform-cassock with shoulder knots-leather baldric and belt-linen shirt-lace and ribbon cravat-breeches with ribbon "cannons"-knit hose-leather shoes-beaver hat with rosette-fabric bandoleer-French-1667

RTW

officer's uniform for hot climate- presumably canvas-all gray with red ribbons-white linen shirt-lace and ribbon jabot- fringed and embroidered baldric-black shoes with gray bowknots-cane and sword- British- 1669

17th Century

grenadier-red uniform lined with yellow-yellow braid with tufted ends- gilt buttons-red cap with fur band-red stockings-black leather shoes-yellow garters-yellow woolen scarf leather belt and baldric-pouch for grenades-dagger- sword-hatchet- British- 1680

infantry uniform- red cassock-gray breeches-gray stockings-woolen scarf- black leather shoes- bearskin cap with braid-edged frontal- leather belts and grenade pouch- powder horn- musket-sword- dagger- English- 1689

dark blue cassock-cuffs, waistcoat, breeches, stockings and baldric in orange-yellow- black beaver cocked hat- black leather shoes-fabric bandoleer-sword- musket- Dutch- 1690

RTW

MILITARY
THE 18TH CENTURY

CHAPTER THREE

FROM 1700 ON, the modern military uniform began to develop in the large European standing armies whereby each country's soldiers and each army's regiments became distinguishable one from the other. The style followed the civilian mode of the day with the color of the coat the predominant feature as, for instance, the redcoat of the Britishers. Certain colors used in facings, collar and waistcoat became regimental distinctions while embroidered motifs in gold and silver, the gorget, sword and sash indicated officers' rank. Of French origin were the epaulettes introduced in 1759, an ornamental insignia of officers' rank copied by other armies. Epaulettes also proved a source of protection against sword cuts and held shoulder belts in place.

The French regiments were dressed in various shades of brown accented with brilliant colors which designated the different regiments and added greatly to the military display. Officers continued to take the liberty of wearing mourning, a privilege accorded the French Guard. An officer might be seen leading his troops, he in all-black except for the gorget hung round his neck. When the soldier early in the period buttoned back the skirts of his coat to permit freedom of action, he little knew he was creating a men's fashion which would survive to this day in civilian life in the full dress tail coat.

All military units in the European armies were affected by the successes of the Prussians in the Silesian Wars, 1740 to 1744, and the Seven Years' War, 1756 to 1763. The latter was the European phase of the French and Indian War in America. The uniforms of the Hussars, originally Turkish, influenced cavalry dress when Frederick the Great employed a regiment of auxiliaries, the Hungarian light horse troops. Their uniform was a handsome, storybook style which ignored comfort completely. It was a tight tunic or jacket with horizontal rows of braid from neck to waist in front, high stock collar, fur cuffs, tight breeches, high, fitted boots and a dolman hanging from one shoulder. The dashing costume appeared in many characteristic variations of the original right up to the nineteenth century, worn even in our own Civil War.

The European standing armies of mercenaries were eventually converted into units to which the provincial militia was added. Till the eighteenth century much laxity existed in uniforms with the exception of those of the Prussians. England, France, Germany and Austria adopted a more practical soldiers' dress with the Prussian drill becoming the model for training and tactics. A visitor to Prussia writing in 1729 says, "The Prussians have a custom which has never been practiced by any troops; to refurnish anew each year. Unity reigns in all details in the army even to the shoe buckles."

In England it was every man's duty to bear arms or else bear the expense of maintaining a soldier in service and with such a background the colonists came here to protect and fight if need be. Although the Colonies did not have regiments of soldiers, each city had its provincial militia while a few larger cities were equipped with independent companies. With the exception of the Quakers and the Dutch of Manhattan there were always militiamen ready for an emergency. Men and money were needed for the French and Indian War when it broke in 1754 and it was up to the Colonies to furnish them. This war proved to be the training ground for the American leaders in the War for Independence.

Most of the militia troops consisted of farmers and woodsmen and the real American uniform, except in the case of the independent companies, was that of the hunter and the frontiersman. It was upon Washington's own recommendation that hunting dress was adopted in the campaign against the Indians in Virginia and again at the start of the Revolution. The soldier's outfit consisted of breeches, tunic or shirt, shoes and gaiters and a hat of cloth or buckskin, all brown in color. Brown evolved as the military color of the Colonies as ordered by the Continental Congress because the dye was to be had on every farm and therefore was easily obtained by the cloth manufacturers in the cities.

The hunting shirt, commonly known as the wamus, was pure Americana. It was really a tunic which slipped on over the head or, if open down the front, had no buttons but was thong-laced or held closed by the leather belt.

Light, warm and wind-resistant, the wamus was most generally made of beautifully tanned buckskin. Much dressier shirts were made of "white deer-skin," elkskin which was tanned to a soft, clothlike texture and milky white. Other shirts were of coarse homespun linen or a wool-linen mixture called linsey-woolsey. All skin tunics were ornamented with cut self-fringe but the fabric shirts were dyed blue and trimmed with a yellow-dyed fringe sewn to the garment. The outer seams of breeches were also fringed.

In 1779 it was directed that woolen overalls for winter and linen for summer be substituted for buckskin breeches. This was an order to most men's liking because by 1780, one reads that overalls of "ticken" or ticking, as we call it, was the favored work dress of both army and navy.

The Indian moccasin stuffed with moss or buffalo hair was the footpiece worn by the frontiersman who spent the greater part of his life in the virgin forest. His headgear comprised the slouch hat, a brimmed felt, and for cold weather, the fur cap of coonskin, bear, fox or squirrel. The cap invariably sported an animal's tail hanging in back. The rifle had been in use in Europe for some time but it was noted that the deadly aim of the unmilitary-looking colonial "hunter" was disconcerting indeed to the well-drilled foreign soldier.

The Continental Congress in 1775 decided definitely upon the uniform colors of brown and white and to assess the men for the cost, as was done in England, by keeping back a piece of their pay. But it was difficult to procure cloth. Eventually companies were clothed in whatever color was available and that meant mixed colors in the same company. Sometimes the patriots came upon enemy uniforms which they appropriated and dyed brown or blue. But sometimes there was no time for recoloring the garments and serious errors occurred between friend and foe on the battlefield.

What uniforms existed were those worn by state militias and independent companies, of varied color and British in style. The final choice of color, which did not materialize until the war's end, resolved into blue coat with red facings and buckskin breeches. The ribbon rosette worn from the beginning of the century and usually black, became a general insignia in the military world. After 1775 it was shaped into a small cockade of pleated ribbon and leather and was added as a permanent identifying mark of a regiment. In 1780 the officer's cockade was changed to black with white relief signifying the expected union of the American and French Armies.

Washington upon taking command ordered that officers furnish themselves with cockades in their hats to indicate rank. The colors were to be as follows: red or pink for field officers: yellow or buff for captains: green for subalterns: an epaulette or strip of red cloth on the right shoulder to denote the sergeant: the same mark in green for the corporal. Further, a light blue ribbon across the breast between coat and waistcoat to denote the commander-in-chief; in the same manner a pink ribbon for major and brigadier general; the same for an aide-de-camp. After the order was issued, Washington changed the major general's ribbon to purple.

However, the Continental Army had no uniforms, Congress having little money and no credit and, even if funds were available, clothing and arms could not be imported, the ports of the country being closed. The army lacked not only clothes but arms, ammunition, tents and food. The years 1777 to 1778 were a period of real suffering. The French Alliance and the Marquis de Lafayette furnished a French army, fleet and arms.

Cloth for uniforms was ordered from France and some officers' suits were made in Paris, the uniforms being a copy of the French military. But due to hitches and drawbacks the uniforms did not become a realized fact and many men, in fact the greater number, were in sadly-mended outfits and veritable rags. In 1783 in the absence of red cloth for trimming, orders were issued that the blue coats be faced and lined with white and that white or gilt be used for epaulette, buttons and sword hilt.

As late as 1783 when the cloth had not yet arrived from Europe, Washington ordered the soldiers "to turn and repair their coats". Apropos of this operation, one must keep in mind that the sewing machine did not exist and that all wearing apparel was handmade and therefore not too difficult to take apart, wash, repair and put together again. As a matter of fact, that was the procedure followed in cleaning an outer garment until the arrival of French cleaning establishments late in the nineteenth century.

Our treaty with England after the war created difficulties with France in the last years of the century so that among various changes of the uniforms in 1796, the black and white cockade significant of French and American friendship was replaced by an eagle. Also in 1796 the infantry finally received their red facings and the officers their black top boots instead of cloth gaiters.

When sea fighting with the French, our former allies, took place in the last decade of the century, Congress raised an army of ten thousand men and Washington was again made commander of the army. Though the French attacked our merchantmen, the American officers still favored the French uniform of blue with buff trimmings, cocked hats, boots lined with red morocco, tight pantaloons, red sashes and black silk or velvet stocks. The troops wore stocks of black leather.

In general, the cocked hat was the masculine headdress of the eighteenth century and the hat of the military world. In civilian life it became a mark of gentility, a sign of professional and social rank as contrasted with the lower classes who wore their slouched hat uncocked. The headpiece of the gentleman and the army officer was ornamented with gold and silver galloon, ribbon cockades, lace, ostrich, fringe and plumes. Gold and silver disappeared from civilian dress in the first quarter of the century when its cost became prohibitive. Although a new galloon was invented with the metal worked on one side only, the fad for such decoration had passed, its use now confined to uniforms and livery.

The most popular hat of the century, both military and civilian, was the Swiss soldier's hat, a large comfortable piece that set well down on the head. It really was a bicorne with high front and back flap, the highest point being the spout-like crease in center front. To the French it was the Androsmane; to the English and the Americans it was Kevenhuller of simplified spelling, named after the famed Austrian field marshal, Khevenhüller. An English note of 1753 calls the hat démodé but it lasted in the army into the early nineteenth century. Then there was the "Ramillies cock" with flaps higher than the crown. The sharply turned-up back flap was higher than the front flap which was scalloped out in the center creating a tricorne. The bicorne, supplanting the tricorne of the 1790's, was another phase of the cocked hat. It folded flat so that in civilian life it could be carried under arm to save disarranging the wig, thus its name "chapeau bras," literally, a hat to carry under the arm. It ended up as the ceremonial dress hat of ranking officers of the American, British and French navies, remaining so to the twentieth century.

A distinctive piece of headgear was adopted by the British Dragoons in the 1760's. This was the "jockey cap," a small helmet of black japanned boiled leather with a roach of stiff horsehair mounted on the crown from back to front. It is to be seen in some pictures of the new American Army from the 1780's. Constantly changing were the many designs and colors of the many military bonnets of this period. The iron-skull was still worn under the felt hat in battle. In 1730, the Prussian Grenadier found the large cocked hat a great inconvenience when throwing hand grenades with his long rifle hung in back. The hat with its protruding corners was easily knocked off the head by the musket. This prompted the Prussian emperor to substitute the Hungarian shako, a sugar-loaf hat with high, pointed metal plate, the design so familiar to us in our andirons of the "Hessians of the American Revolution." To give the hat a more martial air the king had a covering of bearskin added. The hat was popular in the French Army where it was introduced by the German mercenaries and worn by the horse grenadiers. The British also wore this miter-shaped cap but of cloth or velvet with the arms and supporters on the frontal embroidered in gold, silver and colors and very handsome it was.

The soldier's bagwig of black gummed taffeta was drawn tight by a string which was concealed under a rosette of the same fabric. In the fashionable world the black tie ends were brought round to the front and tied into a bow. This style was named "solitaire" and was the forerunner of the black silk tie in civilian life. The "pigtail" was a tightly braided queue, sometimes two, spirally wound with black ribbon. The pigtail or whip of the soldier or sailor was often false, made of black leather or chamois with a tuft or "paintbrush" at the end and was cleaned and polished along with his boots. Late in the century it was discarded in civilian life but retained by the military. The end of the pigtail in the United States Army came in 1808.

The Ramillies wig, also a favorite in the army, got its name from the Battle of Ramillies in Belgium in 1706, fought between the British and the French. An English victory under the Duke of Marlborough, the battle gave its name to the fashions of both sexes. In the Ramillies the pigtail was tied top and bottom with black ribbon and sometimes the braid was looped under and tied. Pure white powder appeared in 1703 and consisted of pulverized starch or flour. Curled and powdered hair in the American Army required stores of tallow and flour, a pound of flour being each man's ration per week. Veterans continued to powder long after the fashion had passed. The dressing of his wig was most important in a soldier's life and often when there were too few barbers, a whole regiment of men would tie each other's wigs.

Natural hair had begun to appear in the mid-century, dressed in the black silk bag with ribbon bowknot, young men dispensing with the bag as soon as they grew a sufficient length of hair. Army officers also wore the ribbon-tied queue during the growing stage and if the tail required extra length, false hair was added. French and German regulations designated the two back waist buttons as the point at which to terminate the whip.

The English sailor wore a jaunty version of the cocked hat which was described in a note of 1762 as "a hat with its sides tacked to the crown, the whole pressed flat and looking like an apple-pasty." In the 'seventies first appeared the shape known as the sailor, a hard, round hat with high crown and narrow brim and made of varnished or japanned leather. Late in the century, it became summer regulation for the crew. The English called the hat the "boater" and to counteract the softening effects of the damp atmosphere, the sailor took to varnishing the straw. Of nautical origin is the name of "sennit straw" for the shellacked sailor deriving from seven-knit, a technique of rope-plaiting which the plaited straw resembled.

One finds the sailor of the eighteenth century wearing loose trousers or shorter, petticoat breeches with the short, boxy jacket over a full shirt and sometimes, the large cocked hat atop his tied handkerchief. In this getup, he presents the familiar and picturesque costume of the pirate.

Distinction by uniform was not officially established between army and navy among European powers until 1748 when a marine dress originated in England setting the pattern henceforth for other naval powers. The colors were prescribed as blue and white, thus, the term "navy blue" with braids and embroidery in gold and silver for top officers. White linen became the uniform for tropical wear.

In 1775, eight months before the Declaration of Independence, rumor had it that the British were massing stores of ammunition and powder in the West Indies upon which news the Americans created a marine corps to take care of such matters. But nothing was settled about a uniform until 1798 when a separate navy department was organized and the Marine Corps placed under its command. Green, oddly enough, was the uniform color of the Army and Navy and accordingly the Continental Marines' first costume consisted of a grass green coat with red facings and white lining, white waistcoat, breeches and knitted hose. This dress lasted to 1804.

After the close of the War for Independence and in the last decade of the century it became apparent that our country also needed a fighting unit to guard the Indian frontiers and while the hunter's garb could not be bettered for such service, the uniform of basic blue was the one settled upon for dress and parade.

French
18th Century

hussar uniform copied from the Hungarian regiments-striped silk sash-chausses drawn over white breeches-leather boots and sabretache-furred cap and animal skin pelisse-carried musket, two pistols and sabre-1721

soldier-uniform in brown and gray-lining and facings of brilliant color to distinguish regiments-leather belts-sabretache-chausses over breeches-tricorne with cockade-musket and sword-1721

grenadier-blue coat with red braid-brass buttons-red vest-coattails turned up-cotton spatterdashes-leather belts and grenade pouch-knife-musket-fur cap with brass frontal and pompon-1762

hair braided and turned up under cap

soldier-blue uniform with red facings and trim-blue breeches-light colored vest-coattails turned up-leather belts and pouch-cotton spatterdashes-musket and sabre-black tricorne with silver edge and cockade-1766

RTW

British
18th Century

hair braided
and turned
up under
cap

marine-
red coat-blue
collar-green
cuffs-white belt-
blue and white
striped ticken-
spatterdashes-
black leather shoes
and pouches-green
cloth cap with
embroidery-
musket-
1742

British tar ashore-1744-
blue and white ensemble-
flat cocked hat-
striped vest-tied
scarf-black shoes-
"navy blue" and white
established as marine
dress by the
British Navy
in 1748

infantryman-
red cloth coat
and vest with white
braid-blue facings,
cuffs and breeches-
coattails turned
up-leather belts-
buttoned
spatterdashes-
black hat, pouch
and shoes-sword,
musket and
bayonet-
1742

Hessian
grenadier-green
coat, cuffs and
lining-white metal
buttons-coattails
turned up-buff
colored waistcoat
and breeches-white
gaiters-black shoes-
brown fur cap
with metal frontal-
braided hair tucked
under cap in back-
native of Hesse, Germany
and subject of the
British Georges

RTW

Continental Army
1775-1800

rifleman in white elkskin hunting costume- self-fringe called "furbelows"- black felt hat- black stock- pigtail queue- elkskin overalls- leather shoes- 1777

shirt or "wamus" and breeches of buckskin- shirt dyed brown- self-fringe- shirt held closed by belt- black felt tricorne- pigtail queue- leather buskins- knit hose- musket- bayonet- knife- powder horn- cartridge box- canteen- 1775

rifleman in buckskin wamus and overalls- self-fringed-tunic laced at neck with thong- handkerchief tied round neck- raccoon cap with tail- moccasins- rifle- powder horn- cartridge box- canteen and axe.

rifleman- hunting outfit of a ranger- in use by the whole army- buckskin or dyed homespun gaiters and moccasins- white shirt with black stock- rifle- powder horn- cartridge box- canteen- axe.

RTW

uniform of the commander in chief-blue coat with yellow epaulettes-buff waistcoat, breeches, facings, linings and buttons-white lingerie stock and jabot-black tricorne-black silk cockade and silver button-black leather boots with spurs-1775

Minute Man in typical civilian homespun outfit, usually brown-white shirt of flax with falling band-buckskin waistcoat-knit hose-leather shoes-black tricorne-gun and sword-1775

cavalryman of General Washington's Guard-white coat with sky blue facings, lining and waistcoat-white belts-white buttons-turned-up coattails-buckskin breeches-Souvaroff boots-japanned leather jockey cap-red band and buck's tail-black stock-jabot

officer in blue coat with white facings-white buttons-white waistcoat with fringe and sash-silver gorget-black stock with turned-down band-black tricorne-black cockade-buckskin breeches-leather buskins-1775

RTW

Continental Army-1775-1800

the Regular Uniform which was not realized until 1785 - blue with white facings and buttons which varied according to regiment - New York and New Jersey faced with buff - black tricorne - pigtail queue - cross belts - black leather half gaiters and shoes - gray knit hose - rifle - bayonet - cartridge box - canteen

cockade of black silk and white leather - denoting French Alliance

rifleman - blue or black coat - red facings and cuffs - yellow buttons and buttonholes - white waistcoat, breeches, hose and belt - black buskins - "ruffled shirt" - black stock - black japanned leather helmet with ostrich plumes - crossed swords and guns and "Liberty" on frontal - rifle - bayonet - cartridge box - canteen - 1780

rifleman in green - dyed buckskin or homespun banded with fur - white shirt with jabot and black stock - leather shoes - rifle - cartridge box - powder horn - knife - canteen - 1776

trooper or cavalryman - brown coat with white facings waistcoat, breeches, buttons and belt - leather guard boots and spurs - coattails turned up - japanned leather jockey cap with silver band and buck's tail - rifle - cartridge box - sword - 1774

R T W

Continental Army
1775-1800

commander of Rangers- red coat with buff facings and waistcoat- coattails turned up-black stock-white shirt collar- beaded leather belt with tails- leather gloves- japanned leather helmet with feather and beaded band- buckskin breeches and fringed Indian leggings-moccasins- sword-knife-fringed cartridge pouch- powder horn- 1770's

infantry officer carrying espontoon- blue coat- white facings, waistcoat, breeches and sword belt- white buttons with blue loops- white shirt and white stock-black Kevenhuller hat-black buskins-leather shoes- 1780's

gunner with wet swab for cleaning gun after each fire-blue or black coat- red facings-yellow buttons and loops- white stock, shirt and waistcoat-blue striped white ticken overalls-black tricorne-black leather shoes- brown belt and rope to move gun-white cross belts- coattails turned up- 1779

Lafayette's corps of Light Infantry blue coat- white facings, breeches, cross belts and buttons- coattails turned up-japanned leather jockey cap with horsehair roach and fur band-black spatterdashes or full gaiters- rifle- 1782

RTW

Continental Army
1775-1800

cavalry officer-green coat with black facings-coattails turned-up showing black-yellow buttons-buff waistcoat and pantaloons-black leather stock-white frilled shirt-white rifle belt-black japanned leather helmet-green plume-black horsehair tail-guard boots-saber-1799

national uniform-infantry captain-blue coat and pantaloons-red facings and fringed sash-white waistcoat and belt-black stock-red Austrian knots and seams of pantaloons-black leather boots-(hussar, Souvaroff or Hessian)-lined with red morocco showing at tops-black felt bicorne-red plume-black cockade-1795

private in regular uniform-blue coat and pantaloons-red facings and leg stripes-white waistcoat, lining and belts-jockey cap with bearskin roach, white band and plume-blue cockade-bayonet belt-1795

foot guard in bearskin bonnet-metal frontal-red leather pompon-hair dressed in pigtail queue and powdered-1775-1785

officer's black felt cocked hat-edged with white-ribbon cockade-black pompon-powdered hair dressed in club-1780's

general-black felt cocked hat-trend toward bicorne-ribbon cockade-powdered hair-1780's

RTW

Continental Marine-
green coat- red
facings-gilt
buttons-coattails
turned up-white
lining, waistcoat,
breeches, belts and
knitted hose- black
hat with white edge-
black shoes-rifle-
sword-knapsack-
canteen-
1776

dress uniform of
John Paul Jones,
Commodore of
United States Navy-
blue coat
faced and lined
with white satin-
enameled buttons-
gold epaulettes-
black cocked hat with
gold edge-black
cockade-white silk
hose-black shoes-
gilt buckles-
sword-
1780's

sailor or "American Tar"-
blue cloth or black
tarred leather
jacket and hat-
pantaloons of
coarse homespun
or ticken-
knitted striped
shirt-black
neckerchief-
leather
belt-
sabre-
1798

common seaman-
blue jacket of
heavy cloth or japanned
leather-loose open
pantaloons of
homespun or
ticken-knitted
waistcoat over white
shirt-black stock
of leather or cloth-
black felt hat
with plume-hair
in pigtail queue-
leather bullet
pouch and boots-
pistol, knife
and sabre-
1776

MILITARY
THE 19TH CENTURY

CHAPTER FOUR

THE NEW CENTURY witnessed the final display of sartorial splendor in the army uniform of the Napoleonic Wars. Change was to affect the whole idea of warfare because heretofore when the warrior attacked with knife, lance or sword, his conspicuous costume mattered little since actual combat occurred at close range. But as firearms gained power in striking distance, it was found that less brilliant dress in neutral colors could be a safeguard against the enemy's marksmanship.

In 1801 the hair was ordered cut short and whiskers, which had appeared, were not to be below the ear lobe. The cocked hat had given way to the chapeau bras or bicorne for officers, the troops wearing the small helmet of japanned, boiled leather with a roach of stiff horsehair, copied from the "jockey cap" of the British.

The Marine uniform of 1804 changed to a more distinctive dress in the claw-hammer coatee which was copied from the basic French model as adopted by the Army and the Navy. The wearers became known as "Leathernecks" because they wore a black leather stock while the officers wore one of black silk.

In the War of 1812, our second war with Great Britain, the newer army units took on the short-tailed coat or coatee and the shako, while the veterans of the Revolution retained the long-tailed coat and chapeau bras as was their prerogative. Soldiers' dress of the period coincided with that of the fashionable world in coatee, skintight trousers and high-waist shaping the form as much as possible. Even the tall shako was not unlike that of the lady of the Empire mode. There was also an undress coat and a full dress jacket in the Hussar style. As of 1813, the order for social occasions called for knee breeches fastened with gilt buckles instead of strings. Woolen cloth was used for winter and nankeen for summer and it was in this period that the color gray first appeared in the coats and trousers of the riflemen. In 1816 the United States Academy at West Point, too, adopted gray as the uniform color, the men having worn the blue coat prescribed in 1814.

In seamen's dress the sailor collar and the black neckerchief were practical variations on the gentlemen's neck mode of wide collar points and muffled black silk cravat. The wider collar protected the dark blue jacket from the powdered hair and tarred leather queue, the neckerchief also serving as sweat band when tied round the head in true fisherman fashion. Sailors in olden days had time on their hands which many filled with handwork, carving, making gadgets and even sewing. Since regulation stripes and insignia did not become official until 1866, the stars and eagles that appeared before that date were embroidered by the wearer.

The campaign uniform that marched to the War with Mexico (1846–1848), a blue coatee with blue or gray trousers, was a definite stride toward comfort and adaptability to climate and terrain. Thought was being given to freedom of movement and the soft forage cap while not of special martial appearance must have been an easier headcovering to wear in active service. Chevrons appeared in 1847 for all non-commissioned officers. After the war military dress took on a new look in the low, tapered shako topped by a pompon or plume, worn also by the British Army and called by them, the "Albert Shako."

A general order in 1852 changed the trousers from Saxony blue to sky blue because quantities of pale blue cloth were available to the Government at an attractively low price. Brass shoulder scales were substituted for epaulettes. At the same time appeared the jaunty slouch hat in black felt cocked on one side, fastened with an eagle and decorated with gold cord and small black ostrich plumage. A new tunic or coat, really a frock coat of French origin in the 1850's, was of dark blue cloth, a fitted body with full skirt. It was worn by the mounted rifles and known as the "chasseur." A good pattern for horseback but the pleats were eliminated in 1858.

As very little attention had been given to army dress, the Federal Army of the North found itself in 1861 ill-prepared for battle in the War of Secession. Although every village, town and city had its militia, the units were not uniformed in prescribed army color which meant a dark blue coat, gray blue trousers and a dark blue kepi. The Confederates, who also lacked uniforms, decided upon gray as their color in trousers, double-breasted tunic and gray felt hat with a broad brim. European models were copied by both the North and the South and thus it happened that the colorful Zouave dress was chosen and worn by many volunteers on both sides. The picturesque outfit popularized by the French successes in Italy comprised a short, dark blue jacket, full, baggy breeches and either a wide sky-blue or red crushed sash. Even the Italian Bersaglieri had an influence upon the American uniform as well as the belted, red smock worn by the Great Liberator Guiseppe Garibaldi.

A certain amount of laxity in dress was permitted among the volunteer soldiers of the western units where the preference for headgear was for the slouch hat instead of the forage cap. It is a well-known masculine trait to be fond of an old felt hat and in the volunteer units, those men possessed of that peculiarity were permitted to wear what they pleased which usually meant the slouch hat. Another idea which originated among the Northerners and quickly spread, was the small patch of color or insignia device which men fastened to their hats or caps. Also to be seen were hats of all colors and shapes including summer straws. Such pieces of attire came under fatigue or field dress, among them a good-looking tunic or jacket of dark blue flannel, worn belted in smock fashion.

In the first half of the century in this age of machinery there came into use many new and important mechanical inventions for the manufacture of shoes in America, England, France and Germany. A severe test of the machine-made shoe occurred with the outbreak of the Civil War and the tremendous demand for soldiers' shoes. The army brogans or "fadeaways" as the troops called the McKay shoes, proved amazingly durable. "Straights," that is neither rights nor lefts, disappeared and "crooked shoes," first worn by the fighting men, became so popular that they were eagerly adopted by civilians. But there were still only two widths to be had.

The sewing machine patented in 1851 was a primitive piece of mechanism but a wizard in accomplishment as compared with hand sewing. No advertising campaign along modern lines was necessary to introduce the new machine to women throughout the land. With the need of thousands and thousands of uniforms the Government purchased the hand-cranked machines and loaned them free to sewing circles and anyone willing to put together the outfits as a patriotic duty. The manufacturers with their newly acquired knowledge of sizes and measurements prepared vast stocks of clothes for the returning soldier. Having worn the machine-made uniform he knew the advantage of machine-sewing over hand-stitched clothes and not having to wait weeks for a suit to be made up. But he did insist that the creases be pressed out so that the suit would not reveal its ready-made origin.

After the war, epaulettes, sashes and the dressy, black felt hat returned for general officers' wear and shoulder knots for other grades. New in this period was the white cork helmet made from the pith of the Indian sponge-wood tree and first worn by the British Army in India. Very light in weight, covered with white cotton and faced with green, it proved an insulation against the hot sun. In 1879, uniforms for summer wear with white trousers were issued to all troops. After the French defeat at Sedan, the western armies, United States included, took to copying the German uniform, especially the dressy, spiked helmet which hailed originally from Denmark in 1850.

An innovation in army dress of adjusting to climate was inaugurated by the British in the Great Indian Mutiny of 1857–8 when they clothed the native troops in khaki, an Indian-made cloth of cotton, wool, worsted or linen or combinations of these fibers. The term khaki has come to describe field service uniform though it is a Hindu word signifying the color, dusty. Khaki was not available when the Spanish-American War broke out in 1898 and the regular army went into the hot climate in the heavy, dark blue uniform suffering great discomfort. More to the point was the cavalry canvas stable dress which was worn by a unit of expert horsemen and marksmen organized and commanded by Colonel Theodore Roosevelt. These men became known as "Rough Riders" in their sports shirt with turned-down collar, trousers and leggings, all of cotton, and the broad-brimmed khaki felt hat, called the campaign hat.

In the following year, the South African War in which the British wore khaki proved to the military world that the uniform must suit the climate and must camouflage as well as clothe the wearer.

Puttees, also a first of this era, were worn in the Anglo-Indian Army in the last years of the century. They are of East Indian origin, the name "patti," a Hindu word meaning a strip of cloth. It was a legging consisting of a woolen strip wound spirally from ankle to knee.

United States Army
Nineteenth Century

uniform of the commander in chief- gold epaulettes with three stars- blue coat with yellow buttons- buff facings, collar, cuffs and breeches- guard boots lined red morocco, showing at tops- Kevenhuller cocked black hat- white plume- powdered hair- black bag- white gloves- sword- 1799 ○ 1802

infantryman- blue coat and breeches- red facings and leg stripes- yellow buttons-

white lining, crossbelts and waistcoat- black leather cap- bearskin roach- white plume- black medallion with eagle- cropped natural hair- brown gaiters- knapsack- rolled blanket- canteen- rifle- 1802 ○ 1810

infantryman- blue coatee- red collar and cuffs- white lining, braid, buttons and crossbelts- white breeches- black civilian style hat of beaver- napped felt- white pompon with medallion- cropped natural hair- brown gaiters- black shoes- knapsack- canteen- rifle- 1810 ○ 1813

officer- blue coatee with wings- blind buttonholes, herring- bone design- blue lining- black leather sword belt worn over red silk fringed sash- white breeches- black leather shako with gold braid and eagle- white plume tipped red- black guard boots- spurs and sabre- 1813 ○ 1821

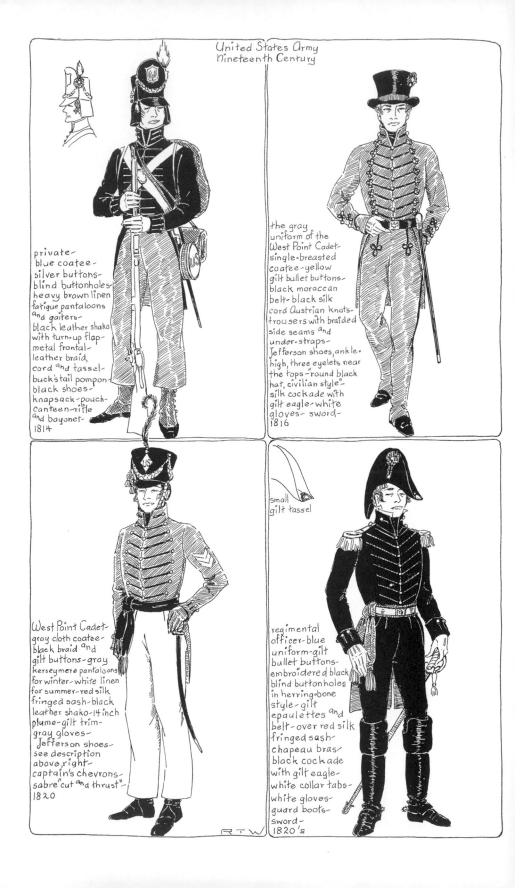

United States Army
Nineteenth Century

private-
blue coatee-
silver buttons-
blind buttonholes-
heavy brown linen
fatigue pantaloons
and gaiters-
black leather shako
with turn-up flap-
metal frontal-
leather braid,
cord and tassel-
buck's tail pompon-
black shoes-
knapsack-pouch-
canteen-rifle
and bayonet-
1814

the gray
uniform of the
West Point Cadet-
single-breasted
coatee-yellow
gilt bullet buttons-
black moroccan
belt- black silk
cord Austrian knots-
trousers with braided
side seams and
under-straps-
Jefferson shoes, ankle-
high, three eyelets near
the tops-"round black
hat, civilian style"-
silk cockade with
gilt eagle-white
gloves- sword-
1816

West Point Cadet-
gray cloth coatee-
black braid and
gilt buttons-gray
kerseymere pantaloons
for winter-white linen
for summer-red silk
fringed sash-black
leather shako-14 inch
plume-gilt trim-
gray gloves-
Jefferson shoes-
see description
above,right-
captain's chevrons-
sabre"cut and thrust"-
1820

small
gilt tassel

regimental
officer-blue
uniform-gilt
bullet buttons-
embroidered black
blind buttonholes
in herring-bone
style-gilt
epaulettes and
belt-over red silk
fringed sash-
chapeau bras-
black cockade
with gilt eagle-
white collar tabs-
white gloves-
guard boots-
sword-
1820's

RTW

United States Army
Nineteenth Century

artillery officer - blue cloth coatee with black trim - gilt buttons - gray kerseymere trousers - sword belt over red silk sash - black stock - white collar tabs - black shako with gilt trim and yellow pompon - deerskin gauntlets - single-breasted gray cloth greatcoat - gilt buttons - first army overcoat · 1828

artillery captain - blue cloth coatee - silver buttons, wings and chevrons - pleated tails - gray trousers - silver belt over red silk sash tied at right side - black shako - silver trim and yellow pompon - gray gloves · 1820's

quartermaster general - blue uniform - gilt trim - buff skirt lining - white collar tabs - aiguillettes - black and gilt belt over red silk fringed sash - black bicorne (chapeau bras) - light blue coq feathers and ribbon - black cockade - white gloves - sword - 1832

artilleryman - blue coatee - gilt trim - gray blue trousers with red stripes - crossbelts - black "tarbucket" with gilt eagle and cannon - red pompon - rifle - bayonet - sword - 1835

RTW

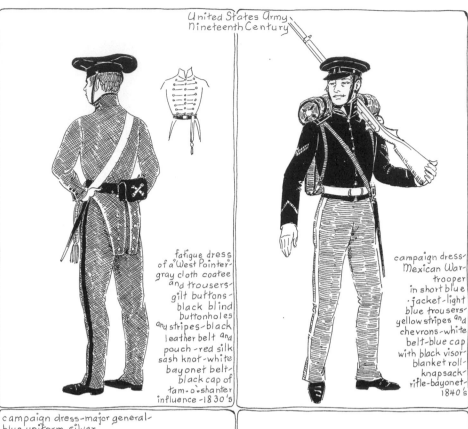

fatigue dress
of a "West Pointer"
gray cloth coatee
and trousers
gilt buttons
black blind
buttonholes
and stripes black
leather belt and
pouch red silk
sash knot white
bayonet belt
black cap of
tam-o-shanter
influence 1830's

campaign dress
Mexican War
trooper
in short blue
jacket light
blue trousers
yellow stripes and
chevrons white
belt blue cap
with black visor
blanket roll
knapsack
rifle bayonet
1840's

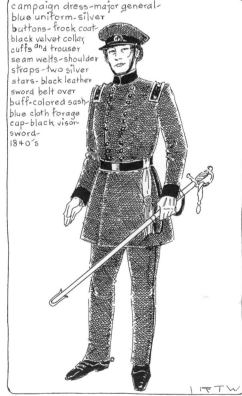

campaign dress major general
blue uniform silver
buttons frock coat
black velvet collar,
cuffs and trouser
seam welts shoulder
straps two silver
stars black leather
sword belt over
buff colored sash
blue cloth forage
cap black visor
sword
1840's

dragoon
foot or mounted
short blue jacket
light blue trousers
with yellow stripes
white belts forage
cap with yellow
band privileges
of the dragoon long
hair, mustachios,
earrings, neckerchief,
pistols and carbine
sabre 1840's

IRTW

United States Army
Nineteenth Century

infantryman-orderly-sergeant-blue frock coat with Saxony blue trim and epaulettes-black leather sword belt over red fringed sash-dark blue cross belts-light blue trousers with green welts-black shako-Saxony blue band and pompon-gilt eagle-sword-1850's

dragoon-field officer in new slouch hat-black felt-cocked right side-held by gilt eagle-gilt cord around crown-three small ostrich plumes on left side-blue jacket with gilt trim-black leather belts-light blue trousers-carbine-1850's

Austrian knots

summer full dress-adjutant-Cadet-United States Military Academy-gray cloth coatee with black braid Austrian knots-gilt buttons-black and yellow chevrons-red fringed sash-white sword belt-white turn-over collar-black shako with coq feathers-white linen trousers-1850's

infantry first sergeant-blue cloth "chasseur" coat with full skirt-gilt trim-light blue chevrons and trousers-black leather belt over red fringed sash-black leather cap box-cartridge box in back-black shako-gilt eagle-blue stripe and pompon-rifle-bayonet and sword-1850's

RTW

United States Army
Nineteenth Century

light
artilleryman-
dark blue cloth
jacket striped and
edged with red-
gilt epaulettes
and buttons-
black leather belt
with gilt buckle-
light blue trousers
pleated in "chasseur"
style-black shako
with red stripe and
pompon-gilt eagle-
saber with black
leather straps-
1850's

cavalry private-
blue jacket-gilt
buttons-black
leather belts-
light blue breeches-
leather boots-
buckskin gauntlets-
blue forage cap-
leather pouch-
sabre-
1860's

corporal-
blue cloth
sack coat or
tunic-turned-down
collar-light
blue trousers-
dark blue welts-
blue forage cap-
black leather
waist belt and
cross belt-others
canvas-pouch,
knapsack,
blanket roll
and canteen-
rifle and
bayonet-
1860's

infantry captain-blue uniform
with gilt trim-up-standing
white collar-light
blue ground in
shoulder straps
and trouser
welts-black
leather belt with
sword chain-
over red fringed
sash-gilt
eagle buckle-
black felt
hat
cocked with
gilt eagle-
ostrich
plumes
1860's

RTW

Confederate States Army
1861-1865

lieutenant colonel-gray cloth frock coat-buff color collar and cuffs-gilt buttons-light blue trousers-leather strap, belt and boots-buckskin gauntlets-black and gray kepi-blue-gray overcoat-sabre

volunteer-gray cloth frock coat-black braid blind buttonholes-collar of varying color-light blue cloth trousers worn over leather boots-leather belt-gray and black kepi-sword

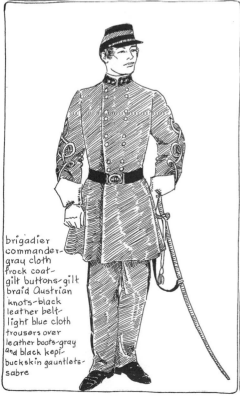

brigadier commander-gray cloth frock coat-gilt buttons-gilt braid Austrian knots-black leather belt-light blue cloth trousers over leather boots-gray and black kepi-buckskin gauntlets-sabre

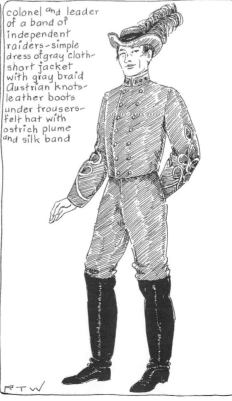

colonel and leader of a band of independent raiders-simple dress of gray cloth-short jacket with gray braid Austrian knots-leather boots under trousers-felt hat with ostrich plume and silk band

RTW

Confederate States Army
1861-1865

member of
independent
company-
gray uniform
with red trim
and stripes—white
canvas belts-
red kepi-
rifle and
sabre

farmer
volunteer-
gray uniform-
leather belts-
felt slouch
hat with
feather-
knapsack-
canteen-
hunting knife-
rifle

Zouave
uniform-
brown
jacket with
red trim-
red shirt-
red kepi with
blue tassel-
blue and white
striped ticking
pantaloons-
black leather
belt over
wrapped red
cloth sash-
leather gaiters-
blanket roll-
knapsack-
canteen-
rifle-
hunting knife

Confederate officer
in pre-Civil War
uniform-dark
blue frock coat
and trousers-
black collar, cuff
stripes and
shoulder straps-
blue kepi-
black leather
belt over red
tasseled
sash-
revolver-
sabre-
knapsack-
canteen

R.T.W.

United States Army
Nineteenth Century

Zouave
uniform in
blue and red-
blue bolero
jacket with
red appliqué-
blue girdle and
sash end edged
light blue-black
leather straps-red fez
(chechia)-blue tassel-
red bloomers-
white gaiters-
leather pouch
and knapsack-
1860's

major general-
blue uniform-
gilt buttons-
black velvet
collar and cuffs-
white stand-up
collar-brown
Russian leather
belt, boots and
sword straps-
steel scabbard-
black felt
slouch hat with
gilt cord-
1860's

cavalry officer in
campaign dress of
the Plains-buckskin
tunic, self-fringed-
buckskin gauntlets-
light blue breeches-
black felt slouch
hat-black leather
boots and belt-
neckerchief for
use in heavy
dust-rifle
and cartridge
belt-
1870's

cavalryman-
blue tunic with
yellow trim-light
blue trousers with
yellow stripes-spiked,
black, yellow-plumed,
black helmet of
Danish origin (1850)-
gilt ornamentation
and long gilt
cords attached left
side and ending
in medallions
and tassels in
front at neck-
black leather
belts-carbine-
sabre-
1870's

RTW

cavalry officer- Plains campaign dress - blue blouse or sack coat - gilt buttons - light blue breeches with red stripes - black felt slouch hat - black leather belt and boots - leather gauntlets - six-shot revolver, sabre and carbine (not shown) - 1870's

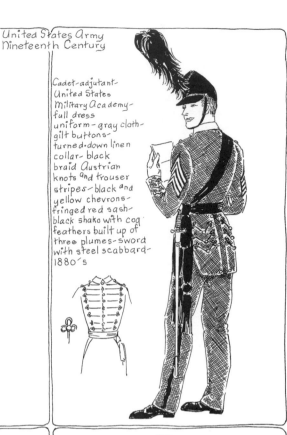

Cadet-adjutant- United States Military Academy - full dress uniform - gray cloth - gilt buttons - turned-down linen collar - black braid Austrian knots and trouser stripes - black and yellow chevrons - fringed red sash - black shako with cog feathers built up of three plumes - sword with steel scabbard - 1880's

summer fatigue dress - infantry quartermaster sergeant - blue blouse or sack coat - lighter blue trousers - white trouser stripes and chevrons - white helmet 1880's

general - full dress blue uniform - black velvet collar and cuffs - white linen collar - gilt buttons and epaulettes - black and gold striped belt worn over gold sash tasseled and tied left side - gilt aiguilettes attached and looped as prescribed - sword - black chapeau bras - black ostrich and ribbon stripe - cockade of gilt and pleated black ribbon 1880's

1, 2, 3 greatcoats-dark blue Melton cloth-black silk Austrian knots-2 and 3, length halfway between knee and ankle-3, belted back-4, enlisted man in French blue-cape lining orange-length to boot top-sword strap enters back vent-1880's

United States Army Nineteenth Century

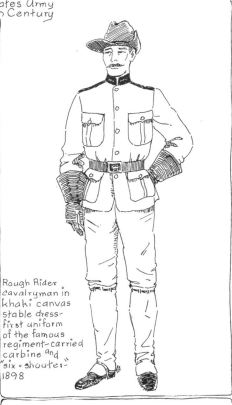

Rough Rider cavalryman in khaki canvas stable dress-first uniform of the famous regiment-carried carbine and "six-shooter" 1898

infantryman-Spanish American War-dark blue cloth tunic-breeches French blue-khaki felt slouch hat-khaki canvas gaiters-leather belts-cartridge belt-rifle-bayonet-knapsack and blanket roll-French blue overcoat-cape lined red flannel-1899

officer wearing the new cap-dark blue and gilt trim-dark blue frock coat with gilt braid Austrian knots and shoulder knots-trousers French blue-trouser crease worn first by army officers in the nineties-leather belt-sabre-1898

RTW

1-1803

2-1804

3-1810

designs in lapels-
navy blue and gilt-
black silk stocks-
white lingerie stock-
white shirt tabs-
center, pearl stickpin-
1, commodore-
2, lieutenant-
3, lieutenant-

officer-
dress
uniform with
black bicorne-
blue cloth
coatee with gilt-
black leather
belt-black silk
stock-white shirt-
white waistcoat-
watch fob-white
cloth pantaloons-
black leather
hussar boots-
sabre-
1812

marine-
navy blue pea jacket-
white drill pantaloons-
white overshirt
with black-striped
collar- black silk
scarf- black leather
belt - hat of black
japanned straw
or leather-
black shoes-
rifle-bayonet-
1812

sailor in hot
weather dress-
white cotton drill
uniform- blue
collar with white
braid-black
neckerchief-
black japanned
straw hat- black
leather belt-
rifle and pistol-
1812

RTW

United States Navy
Nineteenth Century

collars and lapels- commodore- navy blue coat with gilt-white collar tabs-white lawn and black silk cravat- ribbon with order jewel drawn through buttonhole- 1812

marine in navy blue jacket with scarlet facings-white shirt, waistcoat and trousers- gilt buttons- black leather hat with black ribbon- black neckerchief- black leather belt and shoes- pair of revolvers in leather holster- 1813

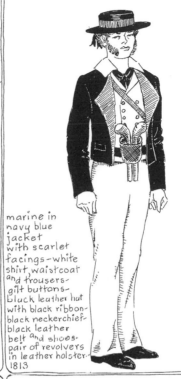

commodore- navy blue coat with gilt- coat invisibly hooked down center front- cockade with order jewel- 1812

captain in summer dress- blue cloth coatee with gilt-white trousers-white waistcoat- lingerie jabot- black silk stock- black leather belt with sabre- chapeau bras- watch fob- black shoes- 1814

captain- navy blue coat with gilt-white lawn collar and vest folds-black silk stock- 1813

commodore- navy blue coat with gilt white lawn collar and vest tabs- ribbon with order jewel drawn through bound slit- 1814

RTW

officer-
navy blue,
double breasted
frock coat
with gilt-
white waistcoat-
light blue
trousers-dark
blue forage
cap-black
shoes-
1830's

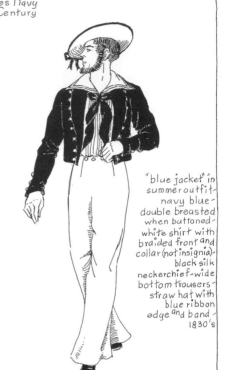

"blue jacket" in
summer outfit-
navy blue-
double breasted
when buttoned-
white shirt with
braided front and
collar (not insignia)-
black silk
neckerchief-wide
bottom trousers-
straw hat with
blue ribbon
edge and band-
1830's

sailors' dress
becoming more
uniform-
ornamental
touches of stars
and anchors added
by wearer-some men
sewed well-blue
jacket and
trousers-white
shirt with light
blue collar and
vestee-black silk
neckerchief-
black straw
hat with
black ribbon-
1830's

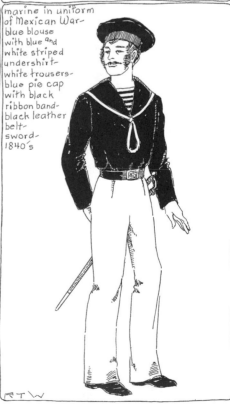

marine in uniform
of Mexican War-
blue blouse
with blue and
white striped
undershirt-
white trousers-
blue pie cap
with black
ribbon band-
black leather
belt-
sword-
1840's

RTW

commodore-
navy blue
uniform-
double-breasted
frock coat
with gilt-
black leather
belt-gilt buckle-
blue forage
cap-
sword-
1840's

marine-navy
blue coatee-
gilt epaulettes-
red and gilt in
collar and cuffs-
red closure edge-
white canvas
belts-gilt
buckles-navy blue
striped, light
blue trousers-
black shako-gilt
eagle and ribbon
band-red
pompon-black
shoes-rifle-
1840's

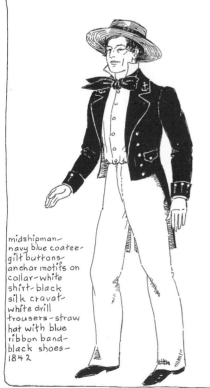

midshipman-
navy blue coatee-
gilt buttons-
anchor motifs on
collar-white
shirt-black
silk cravat-
white drill
trousers-straw
hat with blue
ribbon band-
black shoes-
1842

acting
midshipman-
navy blue
uniform-gilt
buttons-black
silk cravat-
white shirt
collar tabs-
blue forage cap-
black leather
pumps-
1850

United States Navy
Nineteenth Century

admiral-
navy blue
uniform
with gilt-
double-breasted
frock coat-
white collar
tabs-black
silk cravat-
blue kepi
with gilt-
black leather
belt-sabre-
1860's

officer-
navy blue
uniform-
double-breasted
frock coat
with gilt-
white collar-
black leather
belt-blue cap
with gilt-
1860's

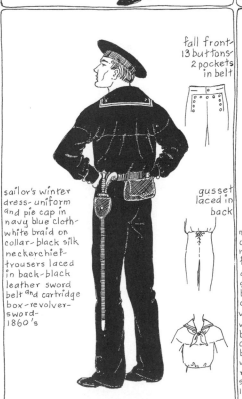

fall front-
13 buttons-
2 pockets
in belt

sailor's winter
dress-uniform
and pie cap in
navy blue cloth-
white braid on
collar-black silk
neckerchief-
trousers laced
in back-black
leather sword
belt and cartridge
box-revolver-
sword-
1860's

gusset
laced in
back

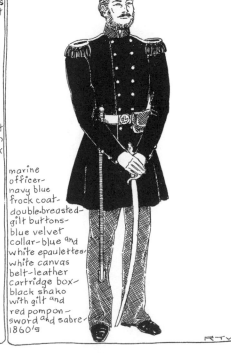

marine
officer-
navy blue
frock coat-
double-breasted-
gilt buttons-
blue velvet
collar-blue and
white epaulettes-
white canvas
belt-leather
cartridge box-
black shako
with gilt and
red pompon-
sword and sabre-
1860's

RTW

Confederate States Navy
1861 • 1865

top-ranking
captain-
gray uniform-
frock coat over
short jacket-
gray forage cap-
black trim-
black shoes

pictures of
Confederate
sailors are
rare- the winter
uniform was of
gray flannel
with black
pie-hat, black
neckerchief and
shoes-
summer dress,
all- white

sailor with sponger
to swab the gun
after each fire-
gray cloth
breeches-
shirt probably
black and gray-
black cap,
neckerchief,
belt and shoes-
bayonet

captain and
skipper of a
raiding cruiser-
nondescript
uniform-
gray frock coat
and trousers-
white shirt-
black scarf
and shoes-
gray forage
cap

RTW

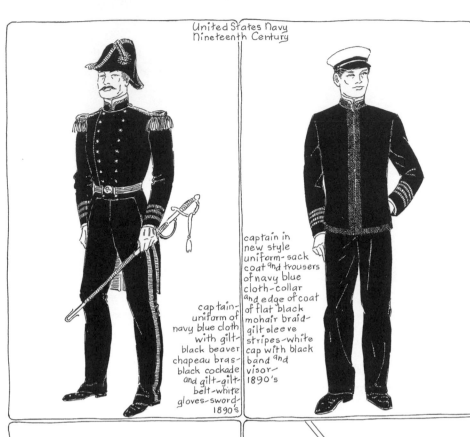

captain-
uniform of
navy blue cloth
with gilt-
black beaver
chapeau bras-
black cockade
and gilt-gilt-
belt-white
gloves-sword-
1890's

captain in
new style
uniform-sack
coat and trousers
of navy blue
cloth-collar
and edge of coat
of flat black
mohair braid-
gilt sleeve
stripes-white
cap with black
band and
visor-
1890's

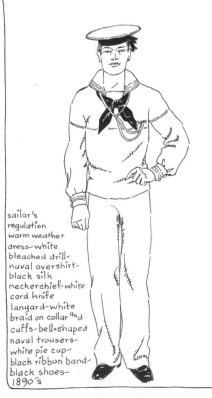

sailor's
regulation
warm weather
dress-white
bleached drill-
naval overshirt-
black silk
neckerchief-white
cord knife
lanyard-white
braid on collar and
cuffs-bell-shaped
naval trousers-
white pie cap-
black ribbon band-
black shoes-
1890's

sailor in
fighting rig
of the Spanish
American War-
navy blue with
black and white-
pie cap-black silk
neckerchief-knife
lanyard-rifle and
cartridge belt-
cotton gaiters-
black shoes
1898

RTW

MILITARY
THE 20TH CENTURY

CHAPTER FIVE

THE UNITED STATES ARMY dress regulations, for the first time in 1902, included the uniform of khaki in field service wear for officers and men in all its branches. According to the climate, it was to be of wool or cotton, the color nearer green than that known as khaki. In design, the pattern followed the British model used in the South African campaign with all overcoats and accessories matching in color. Buttons and designations of units and metal ornaments were to be of bronze-colored metal. The insignia denoting officers' rank was to be worn on the shoulder straps.

The soft, civilian collar devised by the British War Office just prior to World War I and the smart black tie were noteworthy improvements as was the handsome, wide leather belt supported by a narrow strap passing over the right shoulder. This was the Sam Browne belt, a sword belt designed in 1888 by the British General, Sir Samuel Browne (1824–1901). Breeches came to below the knee with leather puttees for officers and canvas gaiters for privates, or puttees of khaki cloth strips bound round the leg such as were worn in the Anglo-Indian Army.

For winter wear there was a double-breasted greatcoat of heavy woolen cloth and a new shorter coat of waterproofed canvas lined and collared with sheep's wool. The hat was that of the Spanish War, the campaign hat in khaki felt. Later, in the war, this hat was replaced by the European style cap which we called the "overseas cap," a snappier-looking headpiece akin to the Scotch bonnet or Glengarry. It could be folded and carried in the pocket. Modern warfare brought back the need of an "iron hat," this time named the "tin hat," a shallow helmet of steel with a padded lining.

World War II carried the army deeply into all kinds of tests and research to enable it to produce the proper kind of clothing to combat not only men and machines but climate and the elements. Cold is a much greater problem than heat and in the Army workshop in Alaska, rigid trials were given equipment, parkas, even the horses' snowshoes. Ski troops were uniformed in all-white and raincoats were worn in artificial, wind-driven storms to be proved water-repellent.

The color of the army uniform was established as "olive-drab" and the brown leather accessories as Army russet color. A lighter shade called drab is used as contrast in the masculine trousers worn with the darker tunic, and the feminine skirt worn with the darker jacket. The overseas cap now became the garrison cap. A new military style was set by the famed "Eisenhower jacket" or, as the British say, blouse. It was designed by a fellow officer, reaching to and fastening at the waist by a self-belt. It had the civilian lay-down collar, deeply notched lapels and two large patch pockets. In a wardrobe of other military clothes, the General has since presented the jacket to the Museum of the Military Academy at West Point. The British approved the blouse and probably for the very first time in their military life borrowed an American idea for soldiering.

Officially, as of 1960, the Eisenhower jacket has been eliminated by a new uniform in greenish-gray cloth with longer and more shapely tunic and instead of tan shoes, socks and belt, these accessories are now black, making a very smart dress. A news item of 1961 stated that Belgium and some other European armies are making use of a permanent trouser crease and said further that the United States Army is following suit. The trouser crease "fore and aft" first appeared in the 1890's when British officers introduced the fashion. To match the outfit, what was the officer's cap in the last war has become regulation United States Army "Class A" uniform cap for all enlisted men. Originally the British cap, we call it the Service cap, a good-looking headpiece with braid band, brass-buttoned strap and leather visor. A gilt disc with spread eagle ornaments the center front.

Many lives have been saved by proper camouflage. Both khaki and olive-drab are excellent neutral colors for the purpose but each one valuable in a different landscape. So the Army concocted a chameleonic one-piece jungle suit, one side olive and the other drab, to be used either side.

Boots were another problem, as it was found that the Alpine boot of heavy leather impregnated with grease was not satisfactory in Alaska. The age-old Eskimo boot of tanned, dried leather with canvas top proved quite perfect for the need because several pairs of warm socks could be worn inside. But the supply of caribou and moose of which the "mukluk" is made was far from sufficient to furnish the Army with the necessary leather and a substitute had to be found. Arctic felt boots are worn by the stationary troops. Another helpful secret of Eskimo and Indian dressing to keep warm and which is being copied is the "layering of clothing," using several light pieces of underclothing instead of one heavy undergarment. The United States and Canadian Armies work together on many problems, solving them in joint research.

For the man who intends to make the Army his career there is a sizable wardrobe to be had in formal, service and field uniforms but if he is in the Reserve or National Guard and enlists just for the duration of war he can eliminate all dress uniforms. During World War II by order of the War Department he was permitted to wear his service uniform as formal dress.

In the Navy up to and during the last war, the officers' uniforms consisted of three classes, dress, undress and service dress and white uniforms for summer use. The blue frock coat with epaulettes and plain belt called for blue trousers, sword and the cocked hat. This is the dress uniform to be worn for particular calls. The same uniform is for undress except that epaulettes and sword were eliminated and instead of the cocked hat, the blue cap was worn. This latter is for reporting on duty or for service at a court martial proceeding. At all other times for which special uniform is not provided, service dress is correct. Whenever ordered, mess dress is to be worn at dinner.

Today, in the United States Uniform Regulations dated 1959, it is stated that service dress uniforms, blue, white and khaki, are the basic uniforms for United States Naval officers and the wearing of a uniform is prescribed or appropriate except when full dress, evening dress, tropical or working uniform is indicated. Full dress uniforms shall be worn upon occasions of state, ceremonies and solemnities by officers in their official capacity. Evening uniforms to be worn at official evening functions at which civilians would normally wear dinner dress or black tie.

Aviation green is worn when engaged in work at aviation activities or at advanced bases when prescribed. Blue to be worn on board vessels and within station limits when weather conditions warrant and when prescribed. Khaki to be worn at sea, at anchorage in isolated anchorages, when engaged in work or aviation activities or when prescribed. Tropical uniforms are worn only in hot weather when considered suitable and appropriate by prescribing authority. And dungarees, when engaged in work which by reason of its nature would unduly soil other uniforms.

In the above regulations of 1959, the dress cocked hat has passed into oblivion. Noted are the visor cap, garrison cap, tropical helmet and the working cap but no chapeau bras after a century and a half of good standing. Epaulettes too, have been supplanted by a new item formerly called scales, reminiscent of armor and now just plain "shoulder marks" which is self-explanatory.

Rumor has had it now and then that the century-old sailor's rig, known commonly among the enlisted men as "monkey suit," was to be re-designed. Only two changes have taken place since the last war, instead of bell-bottom trousers the legs are now straight and the jumper has been shortened. Otherwise, the uniform is pretty much the same, even to the thirteen button, broad-fall trousers. A poll taken among the Navy men of the Atlantic and Pacific fleets in 1956 brought out the fact that though some "city types" wished a new uniform, the majority preferred the British cut set in the sixteenth century and which the American Navy borrowed. Most men thought the side pockets looked tacky and unmilitary, and considered the broad fall front a better fit and more traditionally "navy." Apropos of the vote against a change, a Navy spokesman said that those who man the atomic-powered submarines and the supersonic jet fighters are surprisingly conservative.

Interesting indeed is the heavy rope cord usually gilt, ending in two points or "aiguilletes." We still employ the French word for the decoration though it was "points" in old English. All through the Medieval Period the fashion was to "tie with points" the various pieces of costume, male or female, to fasten the waistcoat, hip-length stockings to the doublet, sleeves to the bodice and finally, tying on pieces of armor. As a military insignia it was adopted in France during the reign of Louis XIII who was king from 1610 to 1643. Today, in our country it is a distinctive mark of the aide to the President at the White House, the aide to top-ranking state officials and the aide to foreign high representatives visiting the United States. It is an important insignia and the various rules to be observed in the wearing of it and the fourragère or both, are several pages long in the official Army and Navy Manuals on uniforms.

In the First World War the fourragère became a significant French military citation and was presented collectively to regiments and units which displayed distinguished service or conspicuous valor in action. The braided cord is worn round the left armscye by all members so honored.

In this day and age women have made a permanent place for themselves in the military forces. Though they have not taken part in active combat, they have established their value as workers to Army and Navy and have been found too helpful to pass by. Of course, the most vital and important service has been in the nursing profession where they have been accepted for over a century but they have also proved adept in many heavy tasks. For instance, in a transportation set-up, women handled not only the office work but overhauled and drove both cars and trucks. The Army and Navy have at times found women better than men in the execution of some jobs that were heretofore considered to be the work of men. The Women's Auxiliary was organized in 1942 but in 1943 the word auxiliary was honorably deleted, the women from then on being created full-fledged army personnel.

There were women in uniform in World War I in about half dozen departments, Nursing, Red Cross, Motor Corps, Signal Corps, Clerical and other non-combat work. But in World War II they acquired real military status, nurses going directly from civilian to commissioned officer rating with a wardrobe of uniforms conforming to those of the men.

Until the last war army nurses have always worn navy blue but they too, changed to olive-drab. Most skirts of the First World War uniforms were ankle-length, an incongruous length for military work whether fashionable or not! Shoes were high and laced, serviceable no doubt, but ugly. By the last war skirts had climbed to the knees, Oxfords were low and still serviceable but much smarter looking. The suits and caps had a dash and an air about them that a top-ranking designer such as our Paris-New York couturier Mainbocher furnished to the American woman in service. Women in the Armed Forces in World War II were much envied by the feminine civilian world. It was during those years that the American nylon stocking was perfected but, by government decree, the glamorous hosiery could only be had by women in uniform.

In general, all uniforms and accessories authorized for enlisted women are the same as those worn by women officers. In a few instances, uniforms for enlisted women below chief petty officers differ from those of the officers. Service dress uniforms, blue and white, are the basic uniforms for enlisted women in the United States Navy. These latter shall be worn on all occasions when the wearing of the uniform is prescribed or appropriate except when full dress, dinner dress, working or a sports uniform is indicated. The service dress light blue uniform is for warm weather. It is generally substituted for service white during working hours when white is not practical, and may be designated as the uniform of the day.

Full dress uniforms shall be worn on ceremonial occasions as is noted for men. Dinner dress uniforms are for occasions when women officers wear evening or dinner dress uniforms. Gray working uniforms are worn in warm weather when white is not practical and may be designated as the uniform of the day. Dungarees to be worn when engaged in work which would soil regular uniforms. They may be prescribed by the commanding officer. As to the sports uniform or exercise suit, the use is optional while engaged in any sport for which the dress would be appropriate.

And now we come to the many, many new inventions in soldiers' service dress on which chemists and scientists have been working, some having passed successful tests in the Korean War, 1950 to 1955. In 1950 a "wet-cold" outfit was issued to the G.I's fighting in sub-zero weather. The undergarments were covered by a water-repellent and wind-resistant field jacket with hood and trousers. The high boots worn over two pairs of woolen socks had thick inner soles. The soldier was kept warm by making full use of the body warmth and controlling perspiration.

A "vapor barrier" uniform which appeared in 1951, fashioned from pliable, molded plastic sponge, rubber-like and about an inch thick, acting as a piece of underwear, provides an inner circulation of drying and warming air. Because of the microscopic cells in the plastic, a soldier thrown into the water with his pack becomes an unsinkable body. The idea behind the suit is that if the soldier is doused, he can without changing his clothes, dry out quite comfortably.

Armor returned to use in the Korean War being worn by Marines and G.I.'s, in an armored jacket made of nylon and fibrous glass. So successful did the waistcoat prove that the Medical Corps recommended its use for all combat troops. It matches the combat uniform, dark green in color, is flexible and does not impede movement. Of overlapping, contoured plastic plates of fibrous glass covered with a special fabric, the vest became standard Marine Corps equipment. Another vest was made of aluminum and nylon encased in canvas. All proved real life savers in stopping bullets at close range, slugs from machine guns and small fragments from bursting grenades which it is said, cause most casualties.

When the Air Force got under way in 1907, it had a long name as the "Aeronautical Division of the Signal Corps, United States Army." One officer and two enlisted men compromised the division and its first mission in its own plane took place one year later. In World War I, the name was changed to Aviation Service and by then it had fifty-five planes and sixty-five officers but only thirty-five were flyers. By the time of Pearl Harbor in 1941, the Air Force had grown tremendously, reaching its peak in World War II. The women of the Air Force, first called WAC's and later, WAF's, in 1948 became a part of the United States Air Force, the legislature integrating the corps into the Air Force Structure.

While this book was being written in the Astronaut Year of 1961, the first American Astronaut made the trip into Outer Space, there and back! He wore the most fabulous uniform of all time, silver blue in color, a full-pressure suit custom-fitted to the individual astronaut. Built into the dress was an arrangement whereby oxygen was pumped into the garment circulating about the body, maintaining an even temperature of seventy degrees. Oxygen was fed into the helmet, the exhaled breath passing out through a vent in the helmet. The suit was also equipped with a communication system.

This was followed by a new fabric for Space travel, a textile surfaced with twenty-four carat gold to protect travelers into the Unknown from the fiery temperatures to be encountered.

As of 1962 the list of brave men who have orbited the earth has grown, all flights being successful; scores of satellites have been placed into an orbit of the earth and capsules have been rocketed to the moon and beyond. Scientists are now thinking of "Space colonies" and planning well-equipped observatories, even way-stations for the travelers, and they say that such plans will call for a hard-shell suit of coat-of-mail to protect the spaceman when riding inside his vehicle or working outside on a platform or a station. Thus research and development programs cover a wide range of technology which is constantly enlarging the frontiers of science and knowledge. In fact, the most fantastic dreams are becoming reality.

U.S.
general-
uniform of
olive-drab cloth-
Sam Browne belt,
boots, belts and
cap visor of
brown leather-
bronze buttons
and insignia-
dress sword

U.S.
colonel-
officer's greatcoat-
olive-drab
beaver or kersey
cloth - self-fabric
belt-bone
buttons-brown
Austrian knots
on sleeves-
campaign hat
with ribbon
band and white
cord tied in
center front-
tan leather
field boots

West Point
Cadet private-
field uniform-
gray cloth-
gray uncocked
campaign hat-
black scarf-
campaign belt
of canvas-
russet leather
shoes-blanket
roll-rifle
1911

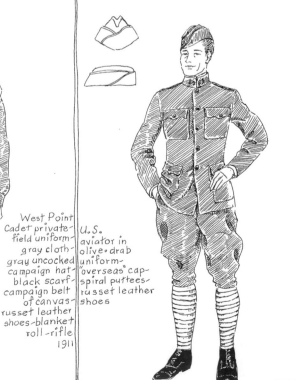

U.S.
aviator in
olive-drab
uniform-
"overseas" cap-
spiral puttees-
russet leather
shoes

RTW

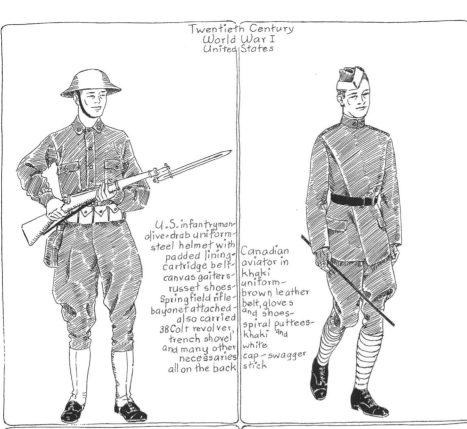

U.S. infantryman-
olive-drab uniform-
steel helmet with
padded lining-
cartridge belt-
canvas gaiters-
russet shoes-
Springfield rifle-
bayonet attached-
also carried
38 Colt revolver,
trench shovel
and many other
necessaries
all on the back

Canadian
aviator in
khaki
uniform-
brown leather
belt, gloves
and shoes-
spiral puttees-
khaki and
white
cap-swagger
stick

decorated U.S. Army
ace aviator-
olive-drab
uniform-cap
visor, Sam Browne
belt, gloves and
field boots in
russet colored
leather-
topcoat with
plaid lining

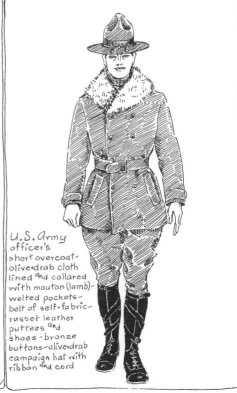

U.S. Army
officer's
short overcoat-
olive-drab cloth
lined and collared
with mouton (lamb)-
welted pockets-
belt of self-fabric-
russet leather
puttees and
shoes-bronze
buttons-olive-drab
campaign hat with
ribbon and cord

R.T.W.

U.S.
sailor in
"blues".
white washable
cap-white
braid on
collar-
black silk
neckerchief-
black
leather
shoes

U.S.
infantryman-
olive-drab
uniform-spiral
puttees-brown
leather belts and
shoes-canvas
cartridge belt
and case holding
gas mask-steel
helmet-rifle

U.S.
Marine with
machine gun-
olive-drab
uniform-
campaign hat-
canvas belts
and gaiters-
cartridge belt-
brown woolen
gloves-russet
leather shoes-
bayonet

U.S. Marine
in "day blues"-
navy blue
tunic and cap-
French blue
trousers with
red stripe-
black shoes-
canvas belt
with bayonet-
rifle

RTW

Twentieth Century
World War I
United States

American
Red Cross-
Oxford gray
uniform-
red marks on
collar-white
blouse-red
scarf-white
cotton gloves-
Oxford gray
overseas cap-
black, laced
shoes

U.S.Women's
Self-defense League-
army-trained-
khaki uniform and
campaign hat-
khaki blouse-
black scarf-
canvas gaiters-
brown shoes

Marinette of the
U.S.Marine Corps-
all khaki
uniform
including
blouse and
scarf-brown
gloves and
shoes

U.S. Signal Corps-
French-speaking
operators
overseas-
navy blue
uniform-
straw or felt
hat in season-
gray gloves-
black, laced
shoes-
brassard
on arm

RTW

U.S.
Army Nurse
Corps-
uniform of
navy blue-
full length
coat over a
"mannish" suit-
white, collared
blouse-blue
straw sailor
hat-blue
ribbon band-
gray gloves-
laced, black
shoes

U.S. Navy
Nurse Corps-
overseas
navy blue
uniform-
hat, blue
felt or straw
in season-
blue ribbon band-
white blouse-
blue scarf-
gray gloves-khaki,
buttoned gaiters-
black shoes

U.S.
Yeomanette-
origin of the
WAVE-navy
blue uniform
including
cap, blouse
and scarf-
gray gloves-
black
shoes

U.S.
Woman's
Motor Corps-
khaki uniform
including
cap, blouse and
scarf-cap
visor, belts,
gloves and
puttees, russet
leather-dark brown
shoes

RTW

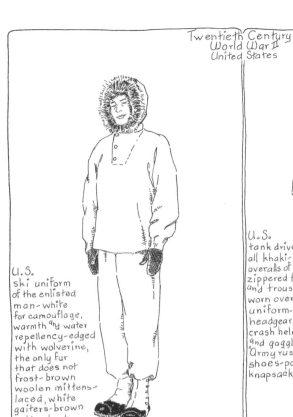

U.S.
ski uniform
of the enlisted
man—white
for camouflage,
warmth and water
repellency—edged
with wolverine,
the only fur
that does not
frost—brown
woolen mittens—
laced, white
gaiters—brown
rubber boots

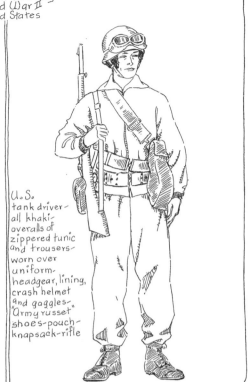

U.S.
tank driver—
all khaki—
overalls of
zippered tunic
and trousers—
worn over
uniform—
headgear, lining,
crash helmet
and goggles—
"Army russet"
shoes—pouch—
knapsack—rifle

U.S.
high-altitude
bomber—
brown goatskin
suit and helmet
lined and edged
with alpaca
pile—mouton
collar—zippered
jacket, inner
sides of legs
and double
boots—boots of
flesh-side-out
leather—lined
goatskin
gauntlets—
goggles on
helmet

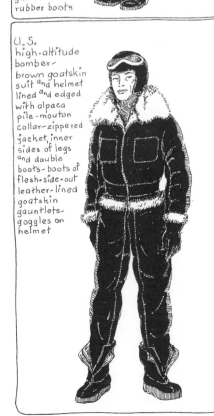

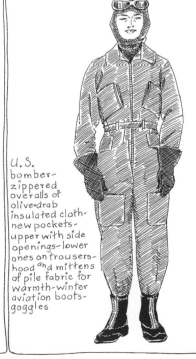

U.S.
bomber—
zippered
overalls of
olive-drab
insulated cloth—
new pockets—
upper with side
openings—lower
ones on trousers—
hood and mittens
of pile fabric for
warmth—winter
aviation boots—
goggles

postwar-designed
uniform for combat
infantry-olive-drab
cloth overalls-
cream-colored
shirt and scarf-
zipper instead
of buttons-army
russet shoes-
steel helmet-
cartridge belt-
rifle and
bayonet-
1949

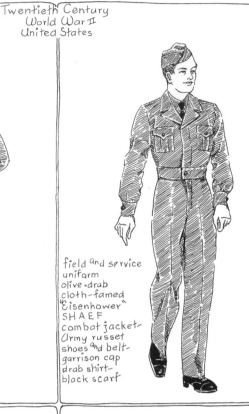

field and service
uniform
olive-drab
cloth-famed
"Eisenhower"
SHAEF
combat jacket-
army russet
shoes and belt-
garrison cap
drab shirt-
black scarf

officer's regular
service uniform-
tunic, olive-drab-
gilt buttons-
trousers of drab,
(light shade)-
drab shirt-
black scarf-
army russet
cap visor,
Sam Browne
belt and shoes

cold weather
battle dress in
paratrooper style-
worn over woolen
shirt and trousers-
dark green water-
repellant cotton-
inside drawstring
instead of belt-
large pocket
on each leg-
lined sateen cap-
combat boots,
flesh-side-out leather
and leather cuffs

RTW

Paratrooper
carrying his
parachute pack-
dress of green
fabric, wind and
water-repellent-
crash helmet-
fur-lined
rubber boots-
note binocular
case

"Leatherneck"
in uniform
for shipboard
duty-"Undress
Blues"- navy
blue tunic-
French blue
trousers-
blue and
white cap-
black
shoes

Marine uniform
of olive-drab-
belt of self-fabric-
light drab shirt-
black scarf
and shoes-
garrison cap

Marine wearing gas mask
for charging through
a smoke screen-
khaki cotton
combat dress-
1950

officer-
bridge coat-
navy blue
cloth-gilt
buttons-
welted
pockets-blue
cap with
black band-
black visor-
white shirt-
black scarf-
black shoes-

Navy or
Coast Guard
officer in
service blue-
white shirt-
black scarf-
blue cap with
black braid-
black shoes-
gilt buttons

sleeve marks-
Navy-star-
Coast Guard-shield

officer-
naval aviation
working uniform
of forestry green
cotton or elastique-
cap cover to
match-shirt of
matching, lighter
fabric-black
scarf- black
sleeve stripes-
brown shoes

officer-
life-preserver
greatcoat-navy
blue water-proof
cotton gabardine,
interlined-bone
buttons-to keep
wearer afloat
for 72 hours-
blue trousers-
blue cap with
black band-
black shoes

RTW

Twentieth Century
World War II
United States

U.S. naval officer—service or dress white uniform—cotton twill or tropical fabric—gilt buttons—white cap—black band and visor—white shoes with plain toe

U.S. cavalry officer's uniform—tunic and cap of forestry green—bronze buttons—drab (light) breeches and shirt—black scarf—cap visor, Sam Browne belt and semi-dress boots of Army russet leather

U.S. officer's Army tropical uniform—khaki cotton shirt and shorts—long, knitted cotton socks—black scarf tucked between first and second buttons—tan, pith helmet lined with green—shoes of Army russet leather

sailor of U.S. Underseas Service (submarine) cap, jumper and trousers of white cotton twill—navy blue welt and dolphins on right sleeve—black silk neckerchief 36 inches square—black shoes

RTW

U.S.
naval officer in
transport coat-
brown goatskin
lined with
alpaca pile-
edged and
finished with
stitching-
mouton collar-
zippered
closure on
right side-
zippered
dispatch
pocket on
chest-
self-belt

U.S. Army
corporal-
overcoat,
trousers, and
garrison
cap of
olive-drab
cloth-gilt
buttons-
light drab
shirt-black
scarf-tan
canvas gaiters-
Army russet
shoes-wool
gloves

U.S. Army
man's poncho
of nylon which
served as tent,
raincoat,
foxhole cover,
ground sheet
or bed roll-
boots of flesh-
side-out
leather with
leather cuffs

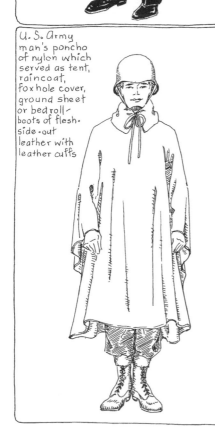

the popular Army
officer's Trench
coat-adopted
from the British-
water-repellent
and windproof-
of tan twill
or gabardine-
removable
wool lining-
self-fabric
belt-
leather
buckle-
bone
buttons-
gun flap
right side
of chest

Medical
Corps
nurse-
white
washable
uniform and
cap-dark
blue woolen
cloth cape-
lined with
maroon
cloth-fastened
at neck by hooks
and eyes-chest by
black frogs-white
shoes and
stockings

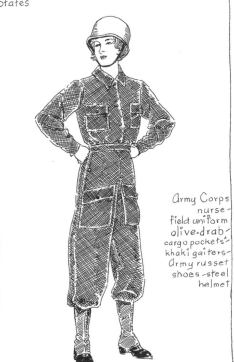

Army Corps
nurse-
field uniform
olive-drab-
cargo pockets-
khaki gaiters-
Army russet
shoes-steel
helmet

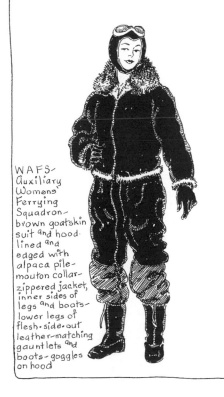

WAFS-
Auxiliary
Womens'
Ferrying
Squadron-
brown goatskin
suit and hood-
lined and
edged with
alpaca pile-
mouton collar-
zippered jacket,
inner sides of
legs and boots-
lower legs of
flesh-side-out
leather-matching
gauntlets and
boots-goggles
on hood

Women Flyers
of America-
overalls of
olive-drab cloth
or cotton-tied
hood-Army
russet shoes

RTW

U.S. Army
Nurse Corps-
regulation officer's
overcoat-olive-
drab cloth-
over one-piece
white uniform-
garrison cap-
white shoes
and stockings-
brown woolen
gloves

U.S. Army
Nurse-
olive-drab
uniform
replaced
navy blue-
tan shirt
and scarf-
brown leather
bag and shoes-
light brown
nylon stockings-
new and available
only to women
in the
Armed Forces

Red Cross
Field Worker-
naval and
Military
Welfare Service
for soldiers here
and abroad-
brown cloth
uniform and
garrison cap-
brown shoes
and bag

U.S. Navy
Nurse Corps-
navy blue
uniform and
"pie cap"-
black ribbon
headband-
gilt buttons and
sleeve stripes-
white shirt-
black scarf
and shoes

RTW

MCWR-
U.S. Marine
Corps Women's
Reserve-
uniform of
olive green
cloth-green
cap with
red cord and
silver insignia-
Army russet
bag and shoes-
light brown
nylon stockings

aws-
American
Women's
Voluntary
Services-
dark blue
uniform-gilt
buttons-blue hat
with simulated
white bowknot-
white shirt-blue
scarf-brown
shoes, purse, belt
and strap-white
cotton gloves-
brown moccasin
styled shoes-
tan nylon
stockings

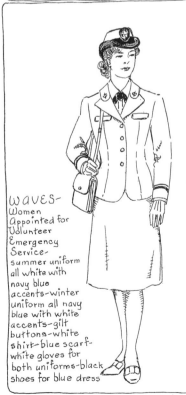

WAVES-
Women
Appointed for
Volunteer
Emergency
Service-
summer uniform
all white with
navy blue
accents-winter
uniform all navy
blue with white
accents-gilt
buttons-white
shirt-blue scarf-
white gloves for
both uniforms-black
shoes for blue dress

WAC-
Women's Army
Auxiliary
Corps-
cap and tunic
of olive-drab
woolen cloth-
skirt of drab-
shirt and
scarf of
beige cotton-
gloves and
shoes in
Army russet
leather

RTW

Royal Canadian Army officer- one-piece battledress- dark brown khaki cloth- drab shirt- brown scarf- pigskin belt with gilt- dark blue cap- brown leather gloves and shoes- spiral cloth puttees

"wren" officer of the WRCNS - Women's Royal Canadian Naval Service- World War II and presently- navy blue and white- black scarf, shoes and black silk stockings

uniform of the Royal Highland Regiment- (Black Watch) navy blue tunic and kilt- gilt lace, buttons and shoulder chains- black ribbon with rosettes on kilt- white belts- sporran of white goatskin with gilt top and black tassels- Balmoral or Blue bonnet with red tuft- blue and red hose with red ribbon garter ends- white gaiters- black shoes

sailor of the Royal Canadian Navy- navy blue woolen uniform- black silk neckerchief- knife lanyard- white undershirt edged with blue- white cap with black ribbon- black shoes

RTW

Twentieth Century
Canadian

machine gunner
of the Cameron
Highlanders of
Ottawa-
one-piece
battledress-
slate blue cloth-
canvas belt-
blue Balmoral
cap-red
pompon-black
leather shoes-
cloth puttees-
1940

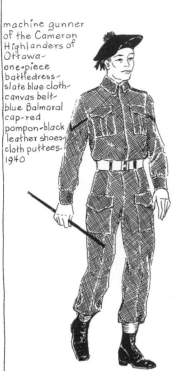

Royal Canadian
Air Force
officer-
uniform of
slate blue cloth-
self belt-
gilt buckle
and buttons-
saddle bag
and bellows
pockets-
white shirt-
black scarf-
blue cap-
black shoes-
1962

uniform of the
Royal Canadian
Mounted Police-
scarlet tunic with
silver buttons-
black breeches
with brilliant
yellow stripes-
black collar and
shoulder marks-
beige felt hat
with brown
ribbon band-
brown leather
belt, cartridge
case and
field boots-
black leather
holster-white
holster cord

a "wren" of the
Women's Royal Canadian
Service-WRCNS-
navy blue uniform-
white blouse-
black scarf-
blue Balmoral-
black shoes-
black silk
stockings
1960

Army Tan
uniform for
summer season-
of Tropical
worsted with
black accessories-
tan service
cap-black
visor lined
with green
leather

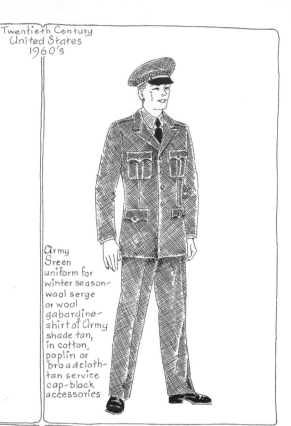

Army
Green
uniform for
winter season-
wool serge
or wool
gabardine-
shirt of Army
shade tan,
in cotton,
poplin or
broadcloth-
tan service
cap-black
accessories

Army Khaki
uniform for
summer season-
cotton uniform
twill-garrison
cap to match-
ribbed, Army
khaki cotton
socks-black
leather belt
and shoes

military
police-
Army Green or
Army Khaki
uniform-
service cap
with white
cover-white
cotton gloves-
black scarf-
black leather
belt and
shoulder straps-
first aid black
leather pouch-
black leather
police club-
lanyard-pistol
and shells-
black combat
service boots

RTW

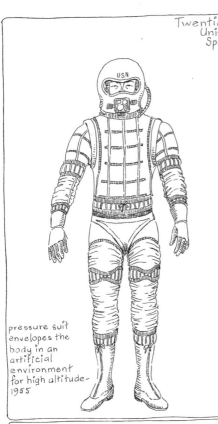

pressure suit
envelopes the
body in an
artificial
environment
for high altitude-
1955

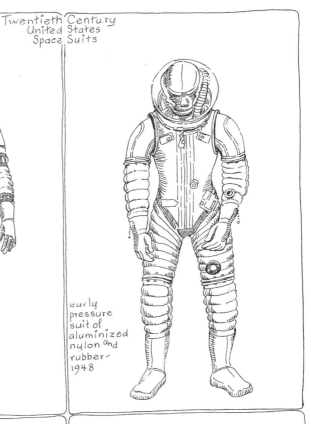

early
pressure
suit of
aluminized
nylon and
rubber-
1948

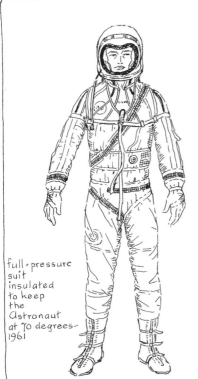

full-pressure
suit
insulated
to keep
the
Astronaut
at 70 degrees-
1961

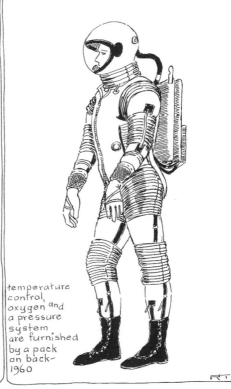

temperature
control,
oxygen and
a pressure
system
are furnished
by a pack
on back-
1960

RTW

THE COLONISTS
16TH AND 17TH CENTURIES

CHAPTER SIX

AND NOW TO THE SETTLERS of the New World, they who came with the vision of a new homeland where they could put down roots and enjoy freedom, worship as they chose, build a future and perhaps even a fortune! From all parts of Europe they came. Much they had to learn and hard they had to work but the result justified the endurance of it all. It became their Promised Land. A virgin continent, they were forced to live in wretched huts of tree bark and earth until each family could build some sort of log cabin from roughly hewn tree trunks. It is supposed that the log cabin was introduced by the Swedes who settled in Delaware.

No doubt the settlers brought some treasures, their clothes and, of course, what tools they could carry. While the men were occupied in carpentry, hunting and fishing for the family's daily living, the women carried on in domestic chores and more. Along with cooking and cleaning they were called upon to manufacture soap, candles, spin, weave and sew, producing all the clothing the family wore. The men learned to dress skins for outdoor clothing and shoes. As the colonies progressed they learned to cultivate flax, hemp, silk, cotton, and wool from Scottish sheep. Especially from the latter, a durable cloth was woven.

In those days, simple well-made clothes of handwoven fabrics lasted a long time due to good-wearing quality and also, because fashions did not change from season to season as they do today. A style sometimes lasted the century and many a fine garment, hat, fur or beautiful lace was bequeathed as an heirloom in a will. Best clothes were worn on special occasions and, of course, to church. At all other times, plain clothes were worn and those are the clothes we shall illustrate. Everyday dress of the solid citizen did follow the basic mode of the period but in a simpler version. The Puritan went to the far extreme in eliminating all ornamentation such as lace, ribbon bowknots, buckles on his shoes, plumes on his hat, whereby, knowingly or not, he achieved a smart and distinctive style.

The first Europeans to colonize in the Americas were the imperious Spaniards who established themselves in Mexico, Florida and California, taking over vast realms by conquest. By 1600 the conquistadors had gained immeasurable lands for the Castilian Crown, added glory to the Church and fulfilled their love of adventure. Gold and silver revenues went to the Crown while the development of agriculture, grazing and commerce produced much private wealth. A New World civilization was the outcome of the combination of Christianity and the ages-old culture of certain South American Indians.

The Spaniards, influenced by centuries of contact with the Moors, were individual in living, art and dress. Their style was elegant and dominated the dress of the European courts for nearly a century. Theirs was the grand manner and they gave to Europe the ruche, the ruff, the corset, the hoop, the bombast style of the padded doublet, trunk hose and, later, the unpadded trunks or full breeches. The knitted silk stocking was a Spanish creation, also the use of rich black as a costume color.

However, over the years, the heavy migration to the New World depleted the population of the mother country and eventually led to the ruin of their industry and commerce at home and consequently to the loss of position as creators of culture. Spanish costume though courtly was not suited to the rigors of everyday life in the new land and was no doubt part of the reason that the Spanish ladies did not accompany their men to the New Spain in the early years of settling.

It seems as if the cape has always been the most important garment in Spanish dress whether the capa or cloak of the man or the shawl of the woman. The masculine cape was draped with a swagger while the feminine shawl and the mantilla lent an air of beauty and mystery to the wearer. With the short cape the gentleman wore the Spanish toque and with the long cloak he wore the broadbrimmed felt hat. The cape was worn in summer as well as in the winter according to the ancient rhyme, "However hot the sun, Keep thy cloak on." And according to season, the fabric changed from silk cloth to woolen serge.

The so-called "Spanish body" required a firm foundation and for this reason men and women wore a leather corset. The board-like silhouette was furnished by a shaped underbodice of hard leather, "cuir bouilli" or boiled leather. It was a fashion that had European gentle folk dieting to acquire the shape, every bit as much as is practiced today.

The Portuguese, busy with their Oriental interests, made little effort in the beginning to colonize the South American territory claimed by them, leaving it to private enterprise to establish trading posts. Colonization eventually followed with the introduction of European cattle, grains and fruits and the beginning of the sugar industry.

The Portuguese, a monarchy of power and wealth in this period, was a mixture of several races, the Latins, Arabs and Israelites. In general their dress displayed the same characteristics as did the costume of Spain and France. It has been said that their wearing of so much black and brown was due to the simple fact that their sheep were either black or brown.

The cape and cloak held the same importance as in Spanish dress and there was the like predominance of black throughout in both masculine and feminine clothes. Usually, their style was much less formal. Portuguese women of the middle class often wore their shawls over the head with the felt hat placed on top, tipping to the front in the very same manner to be seen today among the Peruvian Indians. The separate bodice and short full skirts of heavy cloth bolstered out by many petticoats of many colors have also come down the centuries in South American Indian dress.

The French, who settled Acadia and Quebec, Louisiana and Mississippi, with their innate love of clothes and their talent for sewing, followed the European mode in its essentials in the occasional new costume. But for everyday wear the more colorful and regional dress of their native provinces was what they wore. We are told that was so in Acadia and in the deep south. There is the story of the "Casket Maids" of Louisiana, a group of carefully picked young women, "virtuous and modest," whose emigration was arranged and each supplied with a trunk of clothing, a trousseau in other words.

The Dutch colony of New Amsterdam founded by the Dutch West India Company in 1626 became even in those early days a world center for trade and commerce as well as a cosmopolitan settlement. The ships of many foreign nations were always to be seen in port, many nationalities roamed the streets and many different languages were to be heard in conversation. By 1660 there were about a thousand inhabitants including many English. Many of the colonists who came over with Peter Minuit, the first governor of New Amsterdam, were Walloons. During the Inquisition in Europe, the Walloons or Belgian French had been driven from Flanders and Belgium and had settled in Holland. This group proved as valuable and industrious a community in America as it had been in Amsterdam. In 1664 New Amsterdam was seized by the British and granted by Charles II to his brother, the Duke of York, and named in his honor. Retaken by the Dutch in 1673, it was transferred the following year to the British who held it until after the Revolution in 1783.

The thrifty and industrious qualities of the Dutch combined with their vast privileges as patroons augmented the desire for fine clothes and rich homes. The Dutch were possessed of an individual style of their own but the wealthy burghers and their wives followed the latest fashions of Amsterdam and Paris. When dressed for church or occasions, clothes were rich indeed, having come from the homeland or made of imported fabrics by the Dutch tailors or seamstresses here. They indulged their taste rather extravagantly in accessories and owned many handsome petticoats, the outer skirt often looped up to display the beautiful petite cotte.

Aprons were decorations and made not only of linen or lawn but of silk and wool. The apron had always served a practical purpose but in the sixteenth and seventeenth centuries and well into the nineteenth century it became an exquisite piece of ornamentation. Ladies and little girls of all ages wore an apron of fine linen or lawn, fabrics as costly as silk or velvet and quite often enhanced with beautiful handmade lace.

The elaborate puffed and lace-trimmed sleeves, usually false, were owned in many sets. One certain lady had thirty-seven pairs of sleeves, a real extravagance, and as for caps and ruffs, they cost a pretty penny too. Stomachers when embroidered and jeweled could cost as high as ten thousand pounds. The upkeep was so exorbitant that many ladies did up their own ruffs, no small task to take apart, launder, starch and then repleat.

Men followed the European mode handsomely in baggy breeches, coat and doublet or waistcoat. Leather shoes were for dress but wooden shoes were not unusual for weekdays.

American beaver was the rage and a lure to the exploration of the North America continent and later, to the opening of the West. Beaver was in demand for all manner of costume use but principally for the beaver hat which was the heart's desire of all men and women who could afford the headpiece.

The beaver furnished food and clothing to the Indian but the white man in his greedy hunt for the fashionable fur so depleted the supply that the animal became alarmingly scarce.

Fifteen hundred beaver and five hundred otter skins were shipped to Holland in the very first season of the settlement. Dishonest Dutch citizens tricked the Indian hunters and trappers in trading their precious cargoes for small glittering articles and intoxicating liquor. And so many white men gave up farming for the wealth to be gained in fur traffic that by the 1660's the decimation of beaver in the Hudson River Valley was already apparent. Eventually the Indian fur trade was attracted by the French to Canada so that by the time of the American Revolution fur-trading in Albany had practically ceased. Up to this period the business of supplying peltries to the whites was really the cause of the Iroquois wars against other Indian tribes in their endeavor to monopolize the fur trade.

The English in Virginia, Delaware and the Carolinas wore the contemporary European fashion, practically all dress and home finery being ordered from London right up to the Revolution, especially among the Virginia planters. The ladies and gentlemen of the South adopted the Cavalier style, a graceful mode of silks, velvets, brocades and the large beaver hat. The men wore handsome leather boots with red heels and falling tops. In the picture, too, were long curls, wigs and hair powder along with lace, ribbons and shoe-roses.

The cultivation of tobacco introduced in 1612 was a vital part of the economic and social life of the South. Every family of importance kept charge accounts in London and the purchases made against the foreign accounts were based upon the anticipated crops of the coming season. The Virginians also produced flax, cotton and wool but most quickly acquired wealth with their vast plantations of tobacco grown with the labor of thousands of negro slaves. Slaves were not new, having been introduced by the Spaniards in 1501 in San Domingo, the first seat of the Spanish government in the Americas.

After the Edict of Nantes in 1685 many of the thousands of exiled French Protestants or Huguenots came to America. They settled in Pennsylvania, Massachusetts, the Carolinas and Virginia where they started life anew, at the same time adding their skills to the build-up of the new continent. The everyday working dress of these men consisted of short, loose breeches and jerkin of fustian, frieze or canvas over a shirt of linen or cotton and an apron of dressed leather.

The English settlers of New England founded the colonies of Massachusetts, Connecticut, Rhode Island, New Hampshire and Maine. The Pilgrim Fathers who landed at Plymouth in 1620 were a group of one hundred and two separatists to make the first settlement in New England. The Puritans, another group of separatists, settled in Salem some years later. The mode of the period was the handsome Cavalier style but the Cromwellian Puritans were the ruling power and passed many sumptuary laws while still in England on what to wear. This made Puritan dress the plainest and simplest version of the current fashion.

It was decreed that "Sadd-colours" be worn, grayed tones of any color, no lace, no frills, no shoe buckles or jewels. The man's hair to be cut round, thus the name "Roundhead." The Cavalier wore his graceful, curling locks to the shoulder. The Puritans believed in well-made, sturdy clothes of good material but "playne!" All sorts of fines were recorded for the wearing of ribbons, laces, wide-brimmed hats and what not! Dressier folks wore various styles of capes, particularly in scarlet or with scarlet lining, this color a favorite for two centuries.

The Quakers, known as the Society of Friends, were a company of people who went to Pennsylvania with William Penn in 1682. Of a religious sect founded in 1650, they were mockingly called "quakers" because they trembled when religiously aroused. Though staid and neat, their costume before 1700 followed the fashion of the day in all its color. Quakers wore cloaks of bright hue, especially red, as much as any colonist, calling the favored scarlet cape a "cardinal." Men wore the wide-brimmed hat of Cavalier shape but it was never raised in salute to rank or lady, according to the rhyme—"The Quaker loves an ample brim, A hat that bows to no salaam." The group dispensed with all fripperies of dress yet occasionally did wear wig and powder, even William Penn himself who had a supply of wigs. The feminine headcovering which has come down to us as the Quaker bonnet was the height of fashion in that day and hailed from Paris but the fact that it was worn bare of ornament marked it as the Quaker bonnet. There were no sumptuary laws on record but the seal of approval was for muted color and design of utter simplicity. All garments were beautifully made of the richest silks, finest broadcloth and the sheerest of lawns, and expensive clothes they were! A particular accessory was the green lawn apron and because it was worn so much in the early period it came to be regarded as insignia of the Quakeress.

The Swedish settled Fort Christina, Wilmington today, on the Delaware in 1638 and the German immigration began with the founding of Germantown in Pennsylvania in 1683. Both old settlers and newcomers, German, Swiss and Scotch-Irish entered by way of Philadelphia which was a port from 1715 to 1750. They then trekked southward into the valleys, especially the Shenandoah. These colonists, so many of whom were peasants, became an important and restless society of valuable background with the pioneering spirit. They were all workers, inventors, artisans right down the line to butcher, baker and candlestick maker.

These people, too, followed the European fashion but in a manner which revealed the nationality of the wearer. The German version of the mode was an exaggerated style with great elaboration. In men's dress the over-all effect was decidedly square with slashing covering every bit of space. Women's dress consisted of short, tightly fitted bodice with deep yoke, full sleeves divided into many puffs, long, full skirts and nearly always the apron.

Among the German colonists there were many sects from towns on the Lower Rhine in Europe who settled principally in Pennsylvania where numbers of their countrymen followed. Their costume changed little over the centuries and consisted chiefly of tunic or shirt and trousers and coat made of homespun tow cloth, the cloth woven from a yarn of home-grown flax or hemp. The women's everyday dress was in peasant style, dark colored, a short, full skirt and a tight bodice laced in front over the lingerie shift.

The origin of the modern blouse is in the tunic of the Ancients which became the chemise of the Europeans and in the sixteenth century was especially featured as a decorative part of costume of both sexes. Of fine lawn or linen, plainly made or laced, the garment showed at neck and as undersleeves. Housewife and peasant maid generally wore a long apron to match. It was a fashion that pleased all, male and female, aristocrat and peasant. The making of the chemise meant fine stitchery, an art practiced by lady and farmer's daughter.

Founded upon this, regional dress developed in Europe during the sixteenth century, each province or city creating its own individual dress which did not change with the mode. The women, in particular, brought and wore the costume of their homeland to the new country, even to the wooden shoes. Common footwear for men and women meant the boot, wooden shoes, or barefoot since the leather shoe such as the low, buckled shoe was only for dress-up occasions.

The colonial frontiersman liked his winter cap of raccoon with a tail hanging at one side. Raccoon was in great demand abroad but late in the seventeenth century with the necessity of home manufacture in mind, laws were passed prohibiting the export of the pelts.

The fur muff while not an accessory in everyday dress of common man was a popular enough piece of costume to be mentioned. Not only was it carried by ladies but by gentlemen as well, including some staid dignitaries and court judges. What were at first roomy fur cuffs attached to sleeves turned into small separate muffs of worsted or velvet with fur lining, or a pair of "muffetees." The single large muff was an "indispensable" and its use was not confined just to the young blood but supposedly lent added dignity to the older man of position. An English writer of the time complained of the "strange effeminate age" in which among various other accessories, muffs were used by "gentlemen and others of inferior quality" and also carried by the soldiers of the king's guard.

Men and women wore cloaks, greatcoats and capes varying as to name and of brilliant colors as well as black. Mention has been made of the "cardinal." The short circular cape was the "roquet" as was the short jacket of the mousquetaire. "Rocket" was what they called it in the Colonies. In the seventeenth century, a longer version was named the "roquelaure" after the Marshall Antoine-Gaston Roquelaure of France (1686–1738) whether due to a similarity of names or perhaps because he wore his cloak with a great flare. When the cloak acquired several shoulder capes, it became the "rocolo" to the Colonists. The hooded cape that women wore was the capuchon because of its resemblance to the mantle of the Capucin monks.

In France and England and in the same decade between 1660 and 1670 a great and lasting change occurred in men's dress. The doublet became the vest and the jerkin changed to jacket or cassock. A cravat was worn in place of the falling band. The fancy breeches changed to full knickerbockers bloused over the knees and fastened with ribbon loops. By 1670 the cassock or coat lengthened to the knee, the vest reaching there about 1680. In the 1690's came plain, close-fitting, knee-length breeches concealed by the coat, fastened at the sides by buttons or buckles. The breeches when not of the fabric of the coat were black, which became standard. And there we have the man's habit or suit of modern times.

young girl-always
in all-black when on
the street-face
hidden from view-
never
unaccompanied-
white lingerie
ruff and
sleeve frills-
prayer book
and
rosary-
enveloping
capa, shawl
or cloak-of
fine black
wool

peasant of
Granada-
linen smock-
capa or cloak
of black wool-
black felt
sombrero-
long brown
stockings-
sandals or
alpargatas
of Esparto
rush and
canvas

gentleman
in costume of
silk, velvet
or woolen
cloth-paned
trunk hose-
slashed
leather shoes-
cloak of silk
serge-silk
stockings-
"Spanish toque"
with jeweled
band-lawn
ruff and
sleeve
frills

Spanish lady and
Spanish fashions,
ruff, wasp waist
corset, farthingale
or hoop-gown
of velvet or
cloth over
satin-hanging
sleeves topped
by wings-
white lawn
undersleeves-
lace-edged
handkerchief

RTW

Spanish costume of woolen cloth-slashed colored braid-white lawn ruff-leather belt-velvet bands on pantaloons-black felt sombrero with ribbon band and jewel-black woolen cape banded and collared with velvet-leather shoes-sword

Spanish peasant spinning yarn-cloth frock over lingerie blouse-sleeves tied to armscyes with "points"-braid-trimmed neck-felt bonnet with lappets-girdle carries small knife-leather shoes attached to wooden pattens

Portuguese lady in black dress with multi-colored hand embroidery-lingerie frills at neck and wrists-red cashmere shawl-black felt hat-gloves-soft black leather shoes

Portuguese-black cloth cape with black velvet trim-collar in liripipe style-black felt sombrero-lingerie frills at neck and wrists-black stockings and shoes with latchets-sword

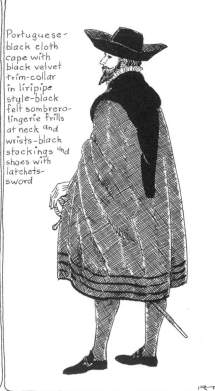

RTW

Sixteenth Century
French
Colonists

lady in fur-
trimmed cloth
gown- or
imitation fur
of woolen cloth-
widow's hood
of dull black
silk lined
with white-
white linen
gorget

carpenter in
working dress-
smock of
coarse linen
or coarse woolen
cloth- tied with
cord belt-
cut and sewn
stockings of
serge or
jersey cloth-
leather shoes-
axe

lady in brocade
gown-white lawn
neck and wrist
frills, yoke and
underbodice-
jeweled
girdle-white
linen apron
indoors, silk
moire outdoors-
escoffian fashion
silk bonnet-
sheer lawn
handkerchief

farmer-
smock-like
garment of
coarse linen
or woolen cloth-
knitted, striped
shirt-cloth
stockings-
leather shoes-
felt hat

RTW

country woman
marketing-
laced bodice and
skirt of wool.
cloth-linen
blouse with
neck frill-
white linen
apron-tasseled
cords-scissors
case, and
sewing bag-
called a
châtelaine-
bavolette
headdress,
fold of silk
attached
to a cap

wine hawker-
woolen
cassock-
cloth stockings-
leather
shoes-felt
hat

country man
marketing-costume
of cloth and velvet-
paned trunk hose
and wings-linen
shirt-tasseled cord
belt-cloth stockings-
silk garters-leather
shoes-beaver hat
with rolled
silk band

peasant carrying
water-simple
dress of woolen
cloth or linen-cap,
apron, collar
and cuffs of
white linen-
hoop to hold
pails in
position-
rosary
at belt

Seventeenth Century French Colonists

peasant living near Paris-handsome dress of her own handiwork-lace and embroidery-cloth skirt-white lawn underbodice-lawn hood over cap-2nd half of century

costume of cloth, silk or velvet-ribbon apron-ribbon loops (canons) on breeches-lawn shirt-falling band-tasseled cord ties-beaver hat with ribbon and ostrich plume-leather shoes with windmill ties and red heels-natural hair or wig-1650

peasant in cloth costume-cassock style coat-petticoat breeches-white linen shirt-cravat of lawn, lace and taffeta-felt hat with ribbon loops-leather shoes with ribbon ties-2nd half of century

peasants living near Paris were often as modish in dress as the Court-costume of cloth, lace and ribbon-fontange headdress-late in the century

RTW

Seventeenth Century
English
Colonists

young woman spinning-woolen cloth bodice, peplum and skirt-muslin blouse and apron-sheer lawn "Dutch coif"-châtelaine holding scissors, sewing and spinning tools

cloth costume in gray, brown or black-falling band and cuffs of lawn with lace points-doublet of muted colors-long silk lapels-felt hat with ribbon band-knitted hose-leather shoes with shoe-roses-1641

velvet or cloth over ribbed silk-lacings over stomacher-white lawn underbodice and whisk (collar)-black hood-2nd half of century

cloth cassock and cape-pockets, buttons and buttonholes-white linen shirt-falling band-beaver hat with ribbon band-leather shoes-ribbon bow knots-2nd half of century

R T W

Seventeenth Century
English
Colonists

velvet or silk gown over quilted undershirt-"ladder of bowknots"-lingerie undersleeves-white lined, black hood worn over a sheer lawn cap-padded shawl-mask for outdoors against cold or sun-late in century

a conservative version of the Cavalier mode-cloth, satin or velvet cassock-satin or velvet vest-full breeches-lawn shirt-cravat of lawn and lace-beaver hat with ostrich-natural colored periwig-silk stockings-leather shoes-ribbon bowknots-mid-century

Puritan-woolen cloth of black, gray, brown and deep, muted hues of most colors-whisk and apron of Holland linen-felt hat worn over Dutch cap-woolen stockings-leather shoes

Puritan in dark-colored cloth-commonly gray, brown or black-gray or green, knitted woolen hose-whisk and cuffs of Holland lawn-black leather shoes with spur leathers-felt hat with ribbon band

RTW

Highland plaid
folded and belted
into baggy breeches
without cutting
the cloth-
leggings of tartan-
saffron yellow
linen shirt-
doublet with
wings-shirred
circular
bonnet-
leather
strap and
purse

striped plaid large
enough to cover
figure and head-
belted at waist-
leather belt with
silver-scarlet
bodice-blue
skirt-head
banded with
snood
silver
brooch-
bare feet
were usual
whether
rich or
poor

two shawls-one plaid-
the other solid color-
over the saffron
linen blouse-
woolen cloth
shirt-jeweled
brooch

early belted
plaid-pleated
sides and
back-plain
ends overlapped
in front-
presumably held
to chest by
hidden belt-
saffron yellow
shirt-leather
purse-dirk, a
double-edged
dagger-claymore,
ancient Celtic,
two-edged sword
with two
slanting
guards

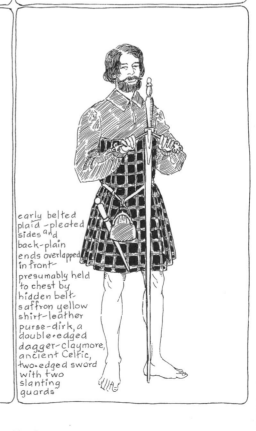

RTW

Seventeenth Century Dutch Colonists

Dutch version of the Cavalier mode- cloth cape- velvet or cloth jerkin and breeches- ribbon loops- falling band with point lace- beaver hat with ostrich- leather boots with muslin boot hose to protect silk stockings

brown cloth skirt with braid trim- black silk bodice- pleated lingerie collar and cuffs- sheer lawn cap with wired edge and jeweled stickpin- pouch and scissors case on cords, "housewife" set or châtelaine

some notes of the Cavalier mode, bowknots with points, and satin garters- cloth doublet with castellated wings and flaps- slashed sleeves- velvet breeches- falling band with cords- beaver hat- silk stockings

cloth or silk costume- bodice with peplum and castellated wings- bowknots on stomacher- lawn ruff and wired cap- muslin sleeves and apron

RTW

Seventeenth Century
German
Colonists

cloth costume-slashed
sleeves showing
lingerie underbodice-
braid-edged
peplum-lawn
ruff with
ties-fur bonnet
of fox-
châtelaine
or "housewife"
carrying
sewing
tools

cloth cape
with braid-velvet
doublet-silk
breeches with
bead fringe-
three-tiered lawn
ruff-silk garters
and shoe-roses-
silk stockings
leather shoes-
leather sword
belt-felt
hat

betrothed peasant
in party dress-green
jerkin with black
braid trim-red
collar and cuffs-
paned wings-
yellow breeches-
green silk garters
and shoe-ties-
black leather
shoes-green
felt hat with
entwined
ribbon
rings

betrothed peasant
in party dress-
costume in green
and red-green
jacket, upper and
lowest flounces-
red collar, cuffs
and lower flounce-
double lawn
ruff-hair braided
with ribbon-
beaded tiara-
green shoe
ties and stockings-
black leather
shoes

RTW

Cavalier mode-green silk
doublet with slashed
sleeves over white
muslin shirt-
brown cloth
breeches-rose
silk garters,
stockings and
shoe-roses-
lawn ruff-
tan gauntlets-
tan leather
shoes-black
cape-black
beaver
hat

peasant in dark
blue cloth costume
with bolero-white
muslin blouse
and apron-
multicolored
embroidered
panel-lawn
neck ruff-
small béret-
hair hanging
in long braid-
black leather
shoes with
ribbon ties

dark green silk gown-
braid-trimmed-slashed
sleeves-self wings-
lingerie underbodice-
lawn ruff-lace
trim at
neck-kid
gauntlets-
fur cap-
black leather
shoes-pomander
suspended
from waist

widow in mourning
dress-all black
except lace yoke
and wimple-
headdress,cuffs,
yoke and
sleeve bands
of crêpe-
undergown
of brocade-
mantle
and gown
trim of
dull silk-
wimple of
sheer lawn
or linen

RTW

Seventeenth Century
Flemish
Colonists

"huke"—Moorish origin-
dates from 11th C.—
worn by European
women
especially of
the Low Countries-
popular 16th
and 17th C.—
of black cloth-
full length-attached
to tiny toque-
pompon-
palatine collar
of lawn and
lace-gown of
silk brocade

black and white
costume-cloth
or silk with
lawn or fine
muslin-apron
edged with
crochet lace-
wired wings-
gold girdle
with
"housewife"
case

cloth costume-
braided border-
palatine collar
lace-edged-
collar, cuffs
and apron
of lawn
or linen-
straw hat
over a
lingerie
cap

negligée house costume-
jacket (samare) of
blue velvet edged with
white fur-satin
undersleeves and
cuffs-cloth or
silk skirt
with velvet
trim-hooded
palatine of
black cloth-
ribbon
bowknots-
laced
handkerchief

RTW

Seventeenth Century
Scandinavian
Colonists

Norwegian
wealthy farmer-
fur-trimmed
cloak with
double sleeves-
belted tunic with
braid trim-
full breeches-
tied silk
garters-
hat of
felt and fur

Norwegian-
French blue cloth
skirt-bodice of
antique yellow-
rose brocaded
silk palatine,
fur-edged-
black silk
border,collar
and cuffs-
large gold
brooch-white
wired lingerie
cap-muslin
apron-gold
girdle with
"housewife"
set-shoes
of flesh-
side-out
leather

Danish-black and white
combination-three
skirts-underskirt
and two pleated-
ribbon sash-
palatine and ruff-
peacock blue
silk bonnet
over black
lawn cap-
gray leather
shoes

Swedish-
buffcoat over
paned doublet
showing
contrasting
colored lining-
full breeches-
fringed silk
garters-tall
felt hat with
bird plumage-
leather sword
belt-shoes
of light
tan
leather

CIVIL DRESS
THE 18TH CENTURY

CHAPTER SEVEN

LIFE IN THE AMERICAN COLONIES by the eighteenth century was one of prosperity and comfort in which fashion became an important factor in general living. Luxuries of all kinds reached our shores, not just from Europe but from China and the Indies. Exquisite fabrics, beautiful china, handsome tapestries, sedan chairs and furniture were a part of the merchandise unloaded from our merchant ships.

"Fashion Babies," dolls about a foot high dressed meticulously in the latest styles, were sent to London from Paris once a month and in this manner the newest whims of the mode were illustrated, just as we today have our fashion journals delivered. The little envoys came on to America from 1750 up to the Civil War and one can well imagine the excitement their arrival created among the women.

In the early part of the century, the American preference was for English fashions, then from 1760 to 1780 both English and French were followed. After that with the exception of the period of the French Revolution, the French mode became the thing in the feminine world, Paris holding the scepter ever since. During the French Revolution, London took over as arbiter of men's dress, a position she holds to our day.

Except for court affairs, English women gave much less thought to dressing than did American women. Letters of foreigners of the times, especially after the American Revolution, comment upon the neatness of the attire of our women but criticize the fact that the wives of bankers and merchants of the New Republic were always dressed in the latest and costly French style. French fashion is considered to have reached perfection in this period. The lovely Watteau gown or sacque named for Antoine Watteau (1684–1721), who created the robe with wide back pleat flowing from neck to hem, is an example of the early part of the century. The hoop or "panier" was the framework worn under the dress. Quilted, wadded or embroidered petticoats were also worn to bolster out the floating gown. The stays or "pair of bodies" continued to be long and slim, made of heavy linen, canvas or brocade and laced in back. The garment was shaped with long stays of whalebone to produce the required look with the bosom pushed up high. Attached to the corset below the waistline were small tabs with eyelets to which the underskirt was laced.

The hairdo which accompanied the Watteau style of costume was charming, simple and close to the head and usually covered by a dainty lawn cap frilled round the face by a lace-edged ruffle. But this lovely fashion was not to last as both coiffure and cap took flight in the second half of the century. There was the elaborately dressed wig to be put on over one's own hair and which could be sent out to the barber to be dressed. This was a convenience to ladies in the colonies who were without hairdressers, a very few of which existed in New York and Philadelphia. A woman, with her head dressed for a ball, done the night before, often would be compelled to sleep sitting up. And very often too, a beautifully dressed head would remain so for a couple of weeks.

But any such arrangement of false hair, flowers, lace and feathers plus pomatum and powder was worn only upon gala occasions—not in everyday life in the home. Hair powder was a fashion for more than half a century. It flattered the complexion, added brilliancy to the eyes and was always used for full dress. A real discovery was the effectiveness of powder as a face beautifier in what sifted over the face when powdering the hair.

Masks were worn in the colonies as a bill of sale of Washington's testifies in an order for masks from abroad for his wife and "Miss Custis." Black silk and velvet were worn in winter while the green mask supposedly protected one from sunburn.

Varied indeed were the many caps and bonnets. From England came the "mob," a cap with deep hanging frill, originally worn by the market women. At first it was called the "Ranelagh mob," then mobcap and finally just plain mob. Bonnets were worn upon all occasions other than full dress and so becoming were most of them that ladies chose to be painted in a cap when sitting for a portrait. The skimmer, a broad-brimmed, low-crowned shape of beaver, felt or straw, was a favorite and often put on over a cap. Such country or "milkmaid fashions" which originated in England were popular in the American Colonies, especially those of straw.

The calash was first made of green silk, later of different fabrics and colors. The material shirred over whalebone or reed hoops could be lowered or raised like a carriage top by a string attached to the front and held in the hand. This bonnet, the very height of the mode, was adopted by the Quakeress in black silk and called the "wagon bonnet."

Bridal gowns and bonnets of costly fabrics such as brocade, velvet and plush were of delicate hue, rarely white. The general use of the bridal veil really dates from the end of the century with the invention in England of a machine for the manufacture of net and lace wide enough for veils and shawls. The first American bride to wear a veil, so they say, was the adopted daughter of Washington, Nellie Custis. Her wedding was held on the President's last birthday in 1799, and her veil, a wedding gift, was a beautiful scarf which she wore pinned to her coiffure.

All classes of men in the Colonies wore the wig although in the South with its warm climate, great distances between plantations, and many poor people, the wig was often discarded in favor of a cap. Men of means wore a cap of fine Holland linen while the commonalty wore a cap of wool. Negro slaves wore half-worn and secondhand wigs, also less expensive ones of white horsehair or goat's hair made up in the simpler styles such as the bob wig. Small boys, too, wore wigs. As noted in the preceding chapter the wig was not spurned by the Quaker who wore a less pretentious one and often was content with his own hair dressed in wig fashion.

Fastidious persons had their wigs especially dressed for Saturday night and Sunday wear and the barbers' boys were to be seen late Saturday afternoons carrying wigs from house to shop and back again. Natural hair began to appear in the mid-century when young men adopted the black silk bag tied with a bowknot of ribbon, discarding the bag as soon as they grew a length of hair.

The cocked hat or tricorne was the masculine hat of the eighteenth century. Generally carried under the arm, "le chapeau bras" became a sign of professional and social rank as contrasted with the uncocked hat of the working class. Meanwhile, in civilian dress in the 1780's appeared an entirely new

128

shape, the tall round hat of felt with rolling brim, a felt napped with beaver, the top hat or "stovepipe" of the next century.

Hatmaking was one of the first of American industries with the men of New York, New Jersey and Pennsylvania wearing domestic hats though importing most of their other apparel. By 1740, exportation of American hats to Spain and Portugal reached such figures that the London feltmakers protested to Parliament against the "outrage" as detrimental to home industry. Forthwith, many restrictions were placed upon the colonial hatmakers.

In this century, the "banyan" of East Indian origin was the common name for a dressing gown. It was the comfortable negligée of man, woman and child in the American Colonies and of bright colored calico, was worn during the heat of summer, especially in the South, to the counting house and when overseeing the plantation.

As ever, women delighted in some new features of costume, be it ever so slight a change, whereas the man in general followed the English pattern. The masculine winter cloak was the greatcoat or perhaps a cape, but as cloth became scarce during the Revolution, American officers introduced the use of Dutch woolen blankets for such garments. In the feminine wardrobe there were short capes for summer and long, padded ones for winter. The pelisse was a fur-lined and fur-edged cloak, often with a deep collar. The roquelaure, like that of the opposite sex, was an enveloping wrap with a cape-like collar. Late in the century, ladies appropriated the smart, male redingote fashion for wear over sheer cotton frocks.

In footwear, clogs and pattens were not only necessary bad weather protection but made it possible for women to traverse the cobbled pavements in fragile, thin-soled slippers. Pattens were fashioned of oak or poplar with leather straps and certainly must have been noisy because notices posted in church entrances requested their removal before entering. Women wore the black leather shoe for everyday dress but slippers with the Louis heel were to be had of colored kid, thin morocco and many fabrics, velvet, satin, brocade, and damask, striped, flowered and embroidered.

The masculine shoe in cowhide and buckskin took on the low broad heel of today in the American Colonies of the 1770's. By mid-century the shoe fastened by means of latchets and buckles and settled down to the colors brown and black, mostly black. For dress wear there were heelless pumps of soft leather and usually black. Boots worn by soldier and sportsmen returned to favor for general wear in the 'seventies. Gentlemen wore light colors for dress in heavy silk stockings, preferably in gray. After 1736, white became general in silk or cotton but in knitted wool for everyday. Women had already changed to white from pale colors in the 1720's.

The shoes of the farmer's family in the American Colonies were still being made in his kitchen over the winter months. All the family took a hand in the work, the men cutting the heavy leather and attaching the soles, and the women binding the edges. The soles were attached by small wooden pegs of maple. The shoes were interchangeable, not shaped right and left. Many a cobbler's bench then used in the farmer's kitchen has today become a collector's piece and is serving proudly in a modern living room as an accessory table.

Some enterprising farmers set up small, ten-foot shops on their property near the house. Such little workshops, each with three or four assistants, soled and finished shoes, the parts of which had already been stitched by the village cobbler. And these tiny wayside shops which produced "bespoke orders" were the very beginnings of the great American shoe industry.

Popular indeed was the woodman's shoe called the "shoepak," the name a derivative of the Lenape Indian word "shipak." It was made like the Indian moccasin without separate sole, ankle-high and of oil-tanned leather, usually white. A heavy boot worn by loggers today in winter was also manufactured and known as a shoepak or "pac."

The working clothes of the laborer consisted of a heavy linen shirt, breeches of striped ticking and a heavy coat of duroy, a coarse woolen cloth. A leather belt held up the breeches which men and boys wore with a leather apron protecting the front. The breeches were made very full and without opening flaps so that when signs of wear defaced the seat, the garment could be turned completely around.

The Revolution, naturally, had a quieting effect in the matter of dress. All costume ornamentation was omitted and articles of foreign make were banned in favor of homemade goods. Jewelry was eliminated and the wearing of mourning set aside for the duration, black cloth having always come from England. Instead, a band of black crêpe was worn as an arm band or on the hat. The Colonists took to wearing camlet lined with green baize for cloaks instead of the fine cloths formerly imported. The men wore garments of tow cloth. In 1789 upon the inauguration of Washington as president in New York, he was dressed in fine dark brown broadcloth, the first made in the United States, in Worcester, Massachusetts. He also wore white silk stockings, silver buckled shoes and a dress sword.

A complete reversal of style had begun to take place in the years preceding the French Revolution, thus meeting a desire for simpler design, less splendor and less class distinction. With the upheaval, magnificence in costume, feathers, hoops, the corset, high heels, paint, powder, beauty patches and all like frivolities became démodé. Paris, discarding these reminders of the aristocracy, adopted the silhouette of the ancient Roman Republic and the chemise à l'anglaise, the English frock of soft cotton, chintz and light silk. The English with their love of country life had already eliminated formality and stiffness from their everyday living and theirs was the dress adopted as the mode.

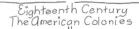

muff
and
hooded
fur-trimmed
cape-
"Manon Lescaut"
in French-
"Nithsdale"
in English-
often
fur-lined-
ribbon
bowknots

double-
breasted
greatcoat or
riding coat-
serge or
kersey-
triple-
caped-
light
waistcoat-
stock with
lace cravat-
black leather
top boots-
uncocked
felt hat-
natural hair
in tie-
2nd half
of century

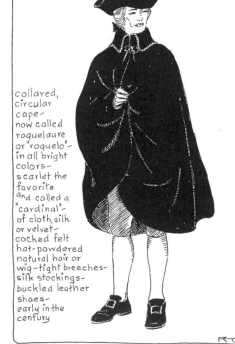

collared,
circular
cape-
now called
roquelaure
or "roquelo"-
in all bright
colors-
scarlet the
favorite
and called a
"cardinal"-
of cloth, silk
or velvet-
cocked felt
hat-powdered
natural hair or
wig-tight breeches-
silk stockings-
buckled leather
shoes-
early in the
century

single-breasted
riding coat-
small cape
and deep cuffs-
leather belt-
tight velvet
breeches-
leather
spatterdashes-
beaver hat-
2nd half
of century

RTW

hunting dress- deerskin cassock- brown leather belts and pouch- high leather spatterdashes- fur cap with turned-up flap-natural hair 1733

the English smock on a Virginian farm-heavy white linen over shirt and waistcoat- colored neckerchief- brown or black breeches- knee-high leather spatterdashes over leather shoes- straw hat- mid-century

Canadian on snowshoes- belted deerskin cassock-felt hat-woolen muffler-leather knapsack, belts, bead-trimmed pouches and ankle boots- knee socks and shorter rolled socks- woolen mittens- natural hair- gun and axe- 1758

French Canadian in fur costume- woolen sash with pouches- tight breeches- leggings presumably of ticking, fur-lined or wadded with cotton-tied at knee- leather shoes perhaps soled with wood or with iron- 1778

RTW

Eighteenth Century
The American Colonies

maid-
cloth skirt and
striped cotton
sacque-lawn
mobcap and
fichu-muslin
apron with
bib-cotton
stockings-
pattens with
wooden soles-
mid-century

negligee or
house dress-
hooded
palatine with
lace and
ribbon-
skirt with
panniers-
silk stockings
and silk
slippers-
1770's

"milkmaid" fashion of
Cromwellian days
revived in 1744
by non-Puritans-
cloth or silk
with panniers-
fine lawn cuffs,
apron and
palatine-
black silk
hood-
buckled
slippers

Quakeress-
cotton or cloth
frock-
lawn cap
with tied
ribbons-lawn
fichu knotted
in back-green
lawn apron-
3rd quarter
of century

RTW

greatcoat
in cassock
style - of
cloth or velvet -
sometimes
fur - lined -
wig or
natural hair -
cocked hat -
silk or woolen
muffler - full
shirt sleeves -
mid - century

workman
in cloth
costume -
brown or
green coat -
neutral colored
waistcoat -
black breeches -
striped knitted
stockings -
muslin cravat -
hair in
pigtail -
straw or felt
hat - mid - century

Merchant

cloth coat -
velvet
breeches -
collar,
lining, and
waistcoat
matching -
lingerie
shirt and
cravat -
wig of
black hair
tied in
back
with black
ribbon -
merchant
1770's

new look
in men's
dress - 1780's -
double - breasted
coat and
breeches
of dark -
colored cloth -
new shaped
hat with band
and buckle -
powdered
hair - watch
fob - top
boots

negligee dress-
Watteau sacque
and petticoat-
satin striped
taffeta with
self ruching-
worn over a
hoop-lace
sleeve ruffles-
lawn cap
with velvet
ribbons-
silk
slippers
2nd quarter
of century

dress of apricot
colored silk-
lawn fichu
and
undersleeves-
muslin apron
with bib
covering
quilted
petticoat-
straw
milkmaid
hat over
frilled
lingerie cap-
velvet
ribbons-
2nd quarter
of century

taffeta mantelet
self-ruched-
crossed in front
and tied in back-
skirt over
hoop-silk
headkerchief
with lace
edge-
1755

forerunner
of a new
silhouette-
pelisse of
cloth or velvet,
fur-lined or
wadded with
cotton-tied
at neck and
bosom-
fur muff-
silk
bonnet
with
ostrich and
ribbon-
1799

CIVIL DRESS
THE 19TH CENTURY

CHAPTER EIGHT

IN THE HALF CENTURY following the War for Independence, the trek westward over the country from coast to coast with the resulting settlements was amazing. In 1848 the treaty with Mexico took place whereby we acquired Texas, New Mexico and California in return for fifteen million dollars and the assumption of the American claims against Mexico. In the same year the discovery of gold was the beginning of the great gold rush. Meanwhile, Yankee clippers and whalers were touching at all important world ports and building a tremendous mercantile empire.

The nineteenth century was new in its many far-reaching phases such as the elimination of class distinction, religious freedom, self-government and a complete break-off from the old idea in many ways.

In France, after her revolution, a new government immediately got to work to remodel the outer face of society by adopting a pseudo-Roman style of dress at which men balked flatly. It was an artistic silhouette but the American women preferred the English version which was simple and modest as compared with almost naked look of the Parisiennes. While the French woman felt that she had achieved the classic look in transparent muslin over pink silk tights and flat-soled sandals, our American women appeared charming in high-waisted muslin frocks over opaque petticoats, as did the English ladies.

Petticoats became a feature of the new costume in lawn, muslin, batiste and mull, short of waist and slim, long skirt, with perhaps several petticoats edged with frills showing below the shirt. In a variation, a tunic of velvet or satin was sometimes worn over the sheath in the winter.

Occasional pictures in the fashion journals of 1805 displayed frilled, lingerie pantalets showing below the skirts. And we find according to a note of 1807 such garments were then being worn, but very often what appeared to be a dainty pair of pantalets were "false drawers," a pair of separate tubes tied at the knees. Women's body linen had ever consisted of chemise and petticoats and the idea of pantalets or drawers was shocking indeed—only dancers had ever worn that garment! Drawers did not become established in feminine dress until the 1830's.

Stays returned about 1811 in the form of a long corset waist fitted to the normal figure and only slightly boned, while a bandeau worn over the chemise held the bosom firm.

The heelless slippers called "Roman sandals" were of kid or fabric, cut very low with ribbons laced across the instep and tied round the ankle.

Of this period was the spencer, a smart little jacket or bolero, open in front and having long tight sleeves. It was most often of velvet in dark color sometimes edged with fur or swansdown. Along the same idea was the little "hussar vest" or canezou except that it went on over the head. There was a great vogue for cotton frocks, especially in white which were worn the year around and under long coats in winter. Cloaks were of such colors as Egyptian earth, pea green and tobacco brown.

The feminine redingote topped by several short capes was typical of the period and so was the witschoura which appeared about 1808. Because the latter was fur-lined it took the Russian name, fur coats having been first worn in Russia. Fur-lined coats became a masculine fashion too, thereby edging out the muff which by 1830 was carried only by women.

An accessory of real luxury was the shawl which became the rage in this period to be worn for more than a century. Shawls though not unknown in Europe and America had never been the mode before, the fashion dating from the return of Napoleon's armies in Egypt. Shawls were large and small, handwoven and embroidered, of silk, wool, cotton, lace or chiffon. Although made on hand-looms in the Orient, beautiful ones were now made in France. From Paisley, Scotland, came shawls woven on power looms, following the intricate East Indian patterns in which "Paisleys" achieved a high, artistic value. The design layout required four months of preparation while the actual weaving on the British power looms was accomplished in a week.

The feminine corset in 1819 acquired a steel busk front fastening and from then on, the waistline decreased in girth. The slim, Empire skirt changed to a bell shape, clearing the ground and revealing the tiny, heelless slippers. The edge of the skirt was stiffened with buckram and often ornamented with rows of trimming. Shoulders were broadened with little shoulder capes, sleeves were stuffed and wired, shaping into the leg-of-mutton sleeve which made its appearance in 1820. Ornamentation was rampant in broad ribbon sashes, large muffs and shawls, shawls in tulle, lace, silk, cashmere, and the ever-beautiful Paisley.

The feminine head was still modish when cropped and scraggly but the most favored coiffure was of classic arrangement. The hair was dressed high and up, off the ears with curled puffs at the temple. Sections of the hair were tightly braided and looped, and to the evening headdress were added artificial flowers, strings of beads, fans of lace, velvet ribbon, gauze or silk and jeweled bibelots.

The Napoleonic-Egyptian campaign was also responsible for the fad of luxurious turbans of brocade, satin, striped gauze and velvet to which were added feathers and aigrettes. Bonnets were fashioned in all shapes and sizes, the poke bonnet or cabriolet hood dominating. Invariably tied under the chin, they were made of fur, plush, velvet or satin for winter and of straw or gauze for summer.

While French refugee dressmakers had gradually returned to France and slowly regained their hold on feminine fashions, English tailors, having seized the ascendency in masculine taste and design, had made London the hub in gentlemen's clothes, a position which it holds today.

It was the English Beau Brummell (1778–1840) who reached the height of society beau and intimate of the Prince Regent, later George IV, from about 1800 to 1812. It is conceded that he raised good dressing to cleanliness, conservatism, a daily bath and daily clean linen.

Bathing was something new and important in 1800. One reads that some ladies and gentlemen in Europe began their day with a bath and changed their underwear once a day. It is recorded that Napoleon and Josephine did that and that the French people thought they bathed too much. To use perfume and toilet water was one thing but to wash with water was, to Americans as well, "that quaint custom of bathing." And, apropos of a supposedly old American custom, we can find nothing on the Saturday night bath until late in the nineteenth century.

In men's dress, the English riding coat or redingote of the eighteenth century developed into the frock coat or cutaway of the nineteenth century. Though today a purely formal piece of dress, in the last century it was a generally worn coat. Pantaloons over soft black boots were also general. With the wearing of sombre hues, the cut of a garment became a special feature. A marked change was to fabric in dark browns, blue and green woolen cloths. And from this period on, the well-dressed man's clothes including hats, boots, even to shoe polish, simply had to be of English manufacture.

An outstanding feature of the early years was the muffling cravat, a bulky affair and very often two cravats, one of fine white muslin under one of black silk. Eventually, the standing collar points in the 1840's began to turn down over the muffler. Then the muffler grew smaller, turning into scarf or narrow bow tie, leaving the collar quite exposed by the mid-century.

An American invention early in 1800 was the detachable collar followed by detachable cuffs and a false shirt front or "dickey." Following up the latter idea in the 'forties shirts were made with an inserted bosom, tucked, pleated or embroidered. The fine white shirt held its own as the mark of the gentleman and remains so in dress clothes in spite of today's vogue for colored day shirts. About 1850 appeared the ready-made shirt and partly made shirts which could be purchased and completed by the home seamstress.

Except among the wealthy who had their shirts made by the "chemisier" or shirtmaker, shirts were usually made at home by the good housewife who spent many hours stitching the handmade garment. The edges of the sheer, linen cambric frills used on the bosom were rolled and stitched into the narrowest of hems and the unending task inspired the writing of that famous poem, "The Song of the Shirt" by Thomas Hood (1778–1845) in which he lamented:

> "O men, with sisters dear!
> O men with mothers and wives!
> It is not the linen you're wearing out,
> But human creatures' lives."

From shirtmaking in the home evolved the commercial pattern of American fame. Women were forever sewing shirts when one husband, a tailor in Massachusetts, had the inspiration of easing the task by cutting a paper pattern for his wife to follow. One of his first patterns to create a demand was of the Garibaldi shirt worn by the great liberator (1807–1882). Exiled for political reasons, Garibaldi sought refuge in Uruguay. In desperate need for uniforms for his Italian Legion, he made use of a discarded supply of red linen found in a warehouse and which the wives made up into men's shirts.

CIVIL DRESS—THE 19TH CENTURY

That was in 1862 and almost immediately Ebenezer Butterick found himself filling orders for friends and neighbors for patterns of shirts, underwear and women's and children's clothes. His sale of tissue paper patterns increased so rapidly that he went to New York in 1865, bought a fashion journal and sold patterns by mail, supposedly the first of all commercial patterns either here or abroad. Orders came in from far and wide, among them an occasional order from England's Queen Victoria.

Elias Howe of Spencer, Massachusetts, patented his sewing machine with grooved and eye-pointed needle in 1848, and in 1851 Isaac M. Singer patented his model equipped with a foot treadle. Followed by the power-run machine in 1865, later a cutting machine, button-sewing and button-hole machines and still other mechanical appliances made it possible, as for instance in a man's shirt, to produce the entire article in a factory.

Ironically, the machine invented primarily to lighten the worker's burden really made a slave of him in building up mass production, longer hours and keeping him a prisoner in the factory where the machines were installed. On the other hand the growth of mechanically manufactured merchandise made for more and cheaper wearing apparel for greater numbers of people. Semi-made pieces became available in the 'fifties, while in the 'sixties practically all items of dress were to be had ready-made and in the stores.

The fitted, corseted look was the fashion for both sexes in the 'thirties and the 'forties, and to accomplish it both sexes wore the corset. Otherwise, in men's dress there were no vital changes. The standard simplicity of their clothes as worn today dates from this period. The changeover of breeches to trousers caused stockings to shorten into socks. Waist and hips were padded to accentuate the shapely silhouette. Jeweled buttons and buckles fastened waistcoats of rich colored velvet with multi-colored embroidery. The exquisitely fine white shirts were collared by cravats, neckcloths and mufflers in color but black satin appears to have been most worn. The Wellington boot was worn under the trousers, a boot cut high of soft, black leather.

Topcoats grew shorter and acquired braid trimming and brandenburg fastenings. An entirely new style appeared in the eighteen-thirties, a box coat of fawn-colored cloth with a shawl collar. Although the new black silk hat was the favorite, top hats of silk or beaver in gray, fawn and white remained in style. To be noted is that the top hat was ordinary day dress for all classes of men in that era.

For the northern gentleman and the southern planter who occasionally ordered domestic clothes, there was the custom tailor proud of his work. An apprentice and then a journeyman from town to town, he had eventually opened his own shop to ply his trade. But there were pioneers, miners and sailors who needed coarse, durable clothing and often could not wait for an ordered garment. And frequently a southern planter wished a shipment of cheap clothes for his slaves and from this need evolved the manufacture of the ready-made. As of the eighteen-thirties the term manufacture meant made by hand.

New York and Boston, because close to wool and cotton factories and sources of cheap labor, became the headquarters where such garments were cut and prepared and then portioned out to farmers' wives and daughters to be finished. The sewing machine made it possible to supply uniforms to the army, to be followed by the enormous demand from the demobilized troops, all this resulting in ever-increasing production, lowered prices and the growth of a tremendous industry. There were those fastidious persons who objected to machine-made clothes and for them garments were partially machine-stitched but fitted and finished by hand.

In the feminine silhouette by 1830, the leg-o'-mutton sleeve had now reached its largest size, from then on gradually diminishing to fall softly over a tight cuff. The dropped shoulder line was accented by berthas, fichus and frills and the high necks were finished with lingerie collar and frill.

By the 'thirties underdrawers had become an essential part of feminine dress causing one to wonder why the garment had not been adopted before. Of merino for winter wear and lace-edged white dimity or colored calico for summer, were pantalets or drawers. The new garment was still quite often false in pairs of ruffles tied at the knees. Pantalets of another style gained a round of notoriety in 1851 when Mrs. Amelia J. Bloomer of Seneca Falls, New York, attempted a reform in women's dress by appearing in full Oriental trousers topped by a tunic or smock. She visited London where she met with a bit of success but little in her native country except that full-styled drawers have ever since been honored with her name, "bloomers."

Five or six petticoats worn under the full skirt presaged the coming of the crinoline which made its debut in the 1840's. At first only a band of braid or horsehair (crin in French), the crinoline evolved into a petticoat, corded and lined with horsehair, and reinforced with a wide band of straw. The procedure of dressing was as follows: if in winter, then first a flannel petticoat, next the crinoline, next a corded calico skirt, over that a pleated wheel of horsehair and finally, the starched, white, embroidered muslin petticoat. A firm foundation!

The full skirt acquired some ten yards in circumference by 1860 and the tight steel corset persisted when the decline of the crinoline began. The Americans devised the "cage américaine" in which the hoops could be raised, making the contraption wearable with shorter street dresses. This was followed by a crinoline with steel hoops from the knees down. In the 'sixties the short skirt brought in taffeta petticoats and by 1869 the bustle replaced the crinoline. The bustle was really a crinoline but the half hoops ran only round the back from side to side. However, women returned to stiffly starched petticoats because the bustle silhouette was created by the bunched-up polonaise.

Bonnets and caps were replaced in 1860 by hats that were fastened to the hair by long hatpins. Caps after a reign of a century retired to the boudoir and eventually were worn only by elderly women.

The hair was dressed in Madonna style drawn into a large cadogan or chignon at the back of the neck and often held in place by a coarse net. It was a classic and beautiful coiffure and in the evening was ornamented with lace, flowers, ribbon, gold and silver nets.

Mantles, shawls, scarfs and fur tippets were still the mode but newer in the flaring silhouette was the full-length greatcoat with leg-o'-mutton sleeves, broad collar and tiny waist.

A glamorous note in footwear was black net stockings worn over flesh color. In the 'sixties appeared high shoes or boots of very soft black leather, black patent leather, kid, satin or a combination of kid and satin. Colored silk petticoats and colored stockings made an appearance in the 'seventies, some stockings with stripes running round the leg, some bright red and some purple with petticoats to match in each case. A lady's best stockings were lisle, with cotton and worsted for common use right to the end of the century. Even in the wardrobe of the wealthy, silk was uncommon, fine lisle thread the smart thing.

The mode of the bustle literally had its ups and downs, declining in the 'seventies, up again in the 'eighties and finally disappearing in the 'nineties. A new style was the fitted, boned basque bodice always made separate from the skirt and worn over a tightly-laced corset.

Deep mourning was observed in women's dress throughout the Victorian Period, an influence of the death of the British Consort and the queen's long retirement from society. It was not unusual for the whole costume of coat, hat and dress to be trimmed with heavy crêpe and the face covered with a black chiffon veil during rigidly set periods of mourning.

Aprons were ever present at home but in the second half of the century "tea aprons" became particularly dainty accessories of sheer white lawn with lovely lace and delicate embroidery.

In the 1840's the masculine silhouette took on an almost feminine air with trousers very tight and the elaborate embroidered waistcoat. Men were turning more and more to black cloth and the frock coat. It was known both abroad and in America as the "Prince Albert," being worn by the Prince Consort of Queen Victoria. During what was termed the "Industrial Revolution," the power and wealth of the middle classes increased greatly and the frock coat, originally the dress of the upper class, was wholeheartedly taken up by "those other people" and quite generally worn. Frock coat and top hat went to church, weddings, funerals and important political gatherings too, eventually becoming everyday dress.

The cut of the coat changed from decade to decade. Another important style appeared in the 1850's in the short lounge jacket or sack coat, a straight garment unshaped by any waist seam. Though at first considered eccentric, it became by 1870 a very popular informal coat and is now more than a century old. Another sack version appeared in England in the 1880's, a short coat without tails intended for dinner wear and dances in country homes. To Americans it became known as the "Tuxedo," because first worn at Tuxedo Park and for some time it enjoyed its greatest popularity in America.

The short box coat so popular here in the 'nineties dates back in Europe to the 1830's. It was always of fawn-colored cloth and always accompanied by a walking stick. In the mid-century and in masculine costume there was also a vogue for shawls. They were worn especially when traveling, long, broad, wide, woolen scarfs in dark colors or plaids folded across the shoulders and over the top coat. Our President Lincoln wore such a shawl along with his top hat.

The top hat was surprisingly tall in an improved model of polished silk or beaver which appeared about 1823, but its popularity dated from the 1840's. Gray, fawn and white beaver remained in fashion with the black silk top hat being relegated to dress wear by gentlemen and for common use by the commonalty. Hats worn with sports clothes were of felt or straw with low crown and wide, rolling brim, a ribbon round the crown with the ends hanging to the neck in back.

A newcomer was the melon-shaped, hard felt hat called in England the bowler and by us the derby, having been designed by the British hatter, William Bowler in 1850. The American name of derby had its origin in the fact that the Earl of Derby popularized the style by wearing the hat to the English races. His model was gray banded with a black ribbon. The hat was quite generally adopted by the 'seventies. In the 'eighties the hard straw hat or "boater" met with approval while the silk topper surprisingly held its own for ordinary wear and without regard to class distinction.

The steam locomotive made travel easier to seaside and inland watering places and mountain resorts, or so it was thought, and thus came about "country clothes." Sports clothes although not so called, first appeared in the 'fifties, light colors in thin silks and washable linen and cotton but, of course, lacking the comfort and freedom of today's "fun clothes." And too, sports clothes were only thought of for men. Heavy tweed suits were to be had, a popular and long-lasting style being the Norfolk suit of the 1880's, a suit which is staging a revival today. A kind of sports sack coat with a belt was worn with knee breeches or knickerbockers. It was introduced as a hunting outfit by the Duke of Norfolk, meeting with approval among Americans as it did with Europeans.

Americans of both sexes became very sports-minded with the women coming to the fore as never before, playing croquet, lawn tennis, golf and taking up bicycling, this latter calling for feminine bloomers and masculine knickerbockers. The settling of the American West produced the wild-riding cowboy. The men who ride the range profited by the centuries of experience of the Spanish and Indians with horses, cattle and the prairies. A traditional dress evolved for comfort and practicability, a dress which is at the same time durable and picturesque in the extreme. And too, it displays a definite spark of Americana.

Here in America, in 1829, one reads of "mixed bathing" at Long Branch only because the rough surf was too dangerous for women to venture out alone, but the writer noted that the bathers were "completely dressed." However, by mid-century the pleasure of sea bathing was an accepted, healthful sport for men, women and children. As late as the 'sixties three to five minutes spent in the water was considered by physicians a long enough time from which to derive benefit. In the last two decades of the century sea bathing was accepted not as a health measure but as a recreation and so thought was given to an appropriate costume.

From Paris in the 1880's came the women's "mannish" tailored suit of cloth, comprising skirt, jacket and shirtwaist. This historical costume event brings to mind a picture of the "Gibson girl" in her smart get-up, the charming creation in the century's last decade of Charles Dana Gibson, the American artist (1867–1944). Her cavalier was the handsome, square-jawed male called the "Gibson man." Due to the immaculate, starched white linen shirts, his and hers, the types were known in song and story as the shirtwaist girl and the shirtwaist man.

The straight-front corset in the 'nineties produced a waspwaist effect, the entire garment heavily boned with steel and whalebone. Humorists dubbed the resulting silhouette the "kangaroo bend or walk." This corseted figure brought in the princess gown of glove-like fit, gored from neck to hem.

Skirts flared at the hem either just clearing the ground or in short trains even for street wear. The underside of the skirt was finished with a narrow silk ruffle called a "dust ruffle." Taffeta petticoats were beflounced with deep ruffles or accordion-pleated frills which swished and made a delightful froufrou when the lady walked. Women wore quantities of underwear in fine muslin and nainsook, handmade, lace-trimmed and threaded with "baby ribbon" of delicate color. Most of it was made by the ladies themselves or by the seamstress who came periodically to the home to "dressmake."

The swan-like neck was collared almost to the ears, the collar boned and usually topped with a ruche. In the last years of the century, the pompadour became the hairdo. To New York from Paris came the "marcel wave," the creation of a Parisian coiffeur named Marcel who with his curling irons arranged even waves round the head. The use of cosmetics was confined to a dash of rice powder, maybe a touch of rouge, but never applied in public. In the summer, even on city streets in New York, a woman carried a pretty parasol to protect her complexion from the sun.

The practice of personal hygiene increased constantly in the second half

146

of the century, many fastidious people of refinement changing their linen daily. But one gathers by reading contemporary beauty hints that those same people actually bathed but once or twice a year. In a manual of etiquette published for ladies of gentility in the 1870's the writer advises that a complete bath once each day upon rising was essential. "Just bathing the eyes" in his opinion was not sufficient, and plain water was preferable but not more than a quart. Reading further, one finds that by the 1880's many were taking a weekly bath, the "Saturday night bath."

As the century drew to a close the bathroom became necessary to gracious living and was installed in more and more homes in Europe and America, especially among the fashionably elegant. We use the word in the singular because one bathroom to a house was luxurious. The famous Tuxedo Club, which opened in 1886 as a most exclusive and sumptuous retreat for social élite, contained one hundred bedrooms but only one private bath.

The century closed on an important note in men's dress—creases in trousers, an idea which had been brewing for nearly half a century suddenly took hold in civilian attire. The Prince of Wales upon his visit here in 1860 wore his trousers pressed four ways, on the sides, front and back. In the eighteen-nineties creases fore and aft as worn by British Army officers were adopted by well-dressed civilians. Trouser cuffs, new about the same time, again were first seen on British Military and again copied in civilian life.

gown of cloth, velvet or silk-ribbon border-ruche at neck and wrists-scarf and tam-o'-shanter are forerunner of coming vogue of things Celtic-ostrich tips- 1812

walking costume-coat of reseda green cloth with black velvet border-beige frock-beige silk "cottage" bonnet with black velvet brim-beige ties and ostrich tips-lingerie ruff called a "Betsie"- black "Roman sandals" 1812

white frock of Indian twill muslin-sage green velvet spencer-white silk collar and lapels-tucked white silk bonnet-black slippers- 1800

maid's costume-striped cotton dress-checked gingham apron-muslin cap with tippet and attached collar buttoned in front-black slippers- 1800

RTW

claw-hammer
tail coat of
gray blue cloth-
buff waistcoat
and breeches-
second
waistcoat of
striped silk,
buff and
white-
putty colored
riding coat-
black silk
top hat-
black boots
with brown
leather
tops-
1802

beige cashmere
frock with
taffeta ruching-
brown velvet
jacket with
brown taffeta
ruching-
fringed beige
shoulder
shawl-white
neck frill-
brown velvet
bonnet with
rose silk
trim-
1819

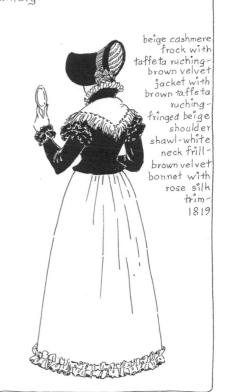

housewife, schoolma'am or
governess-brown, blue
or black wool,
cotton or silk-
tucked yoke
with frill
and scarf-
white muslin
apron-
1825

dark
green
claw-hammer
tail coat-black
velvet collar-
pea green
waistcoat-
fawn colored
trousers-black
top hat-
lingerie stock,
jabot and
collar tabs-
flat black
pumps with
gaiters-
1809

Quakeress of
Philadelphia in
"going to meeting"
dress—all white—
gown of silk
or fine cotton
(like mull)—fringed
woolen shawl—
silk bonnet—
white slippers—
1812

Paisley
shawl in
reds and
Chinese blue—
black ground—
beige dress
with pleated
ruffles—
small black,
pleated
taffeta bonnet—
yellow roses
and buds—
black
slippers—
1814

Quakeress in
thin gray silk
mantle over
white dress—
black taffeta
bonnet—
black
slippers—
1812

Quaker in
"old fashion"
dress—wore
tight breeches
to 1840's—drab
cassimere coat—
black velvet
waistcoat—
nankeen breeches—
"formidable"
black beaver hat—
white shirt, stock
and cravat—white
silk stockings—
black shoes—
silver
buckles—
1812

RTW

frock coat of
tobacco brown
broadcloth
with black
velvet shawl
collar-fawn
colored
waistcoat
and trousers-
over fine
black boots-
black silk
top hat
1831

gown of
plum-colored
taffeta
white
organdie
collar and
cuffs
1830

day costume for
calling and walking-
Russian green
velvet coat-
taffeta bowknots-
embroidered
white linen
collar-fawn
colored silk
bonnet-pink
roses-yellow
kid gloves-
boots of gray
cloth and
black
patent
leather
1835

redingote of
bottle green
cloth-black
velvet collar-
light gray
trousers over
black boots-
lingerie cravat-
chamois gloves-
black silk
top hat-1831

RTW

Bloomer frock-
embroidered
organdie and
black velvetine
bodice-short
skirt with
crinoline-
full Turkish
pantaloons-
neck ruche-
straw hat
with
ribbons-
black
slippers-
1851

brown cloth,
one-button
sack coat-gray
cloth trousers
with brown line
plaid-turned-
down collar-
black silk
cravat- black
hard felt derby-
red velvet
waistcoat-
black shoes-
1861

tailored suit-
French gray
faille-accordion
pleated
underskirt-
yellow silk
waistcoat with
black velvet
edge and
collar-
black felt hat
with yellow
ostrich-
1880's

the
bustle-
costume
in black
and robin's
egg blue-
bodice and
bustle skirt of
black taffeta-
underskirt and
sleeve frills,
accordion
pleated
blue silk-
Dolly Varden
hat with
pink roses
and mauve
ties-
1870's

RTW

gentleman Mexican
horseman-cloth habit-
black jacket with
silver ornaments
and toggles-
dark colored
trousers over
boots-rows
of silver
buttons on
side seams-
white shirt
and cravat-
sombrero
white or gray
with silver
lace band
and
embroidery-
quirt in
hand

frockcoat
of black
broadcloth-
white linen
shirt-wing
collar-black
silk cravat-
black felt
slouch hat-
black boots
and spurs-
1870's

long hair,
sack coat
and nankeen
trousers-
brown woolen
jacket-white
linen shirt-
bright-colored
neckerchief-
leather belt
and boots-
ten-gallon
hat-
1880's

black cloth
waistcoat-
linen shirt-
indigo blue
denim "levis"-
black leather
boots-tan felt
Stetson-
cartridge
belt with
Mexican
holster-
1890's

RTW

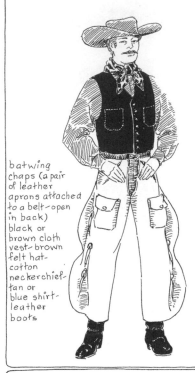

batwing chaps (a pair of leather aprons attached to a belt—open in back) black or brown cloth vest—brown felt hat—cotton neckerchief—tan or blue shirt—leather boots

traditional leather chaps over blue or brown denim pants—pants legs turned up over leather boots—cotton shirt—bright colored neckerchief—light brown felt or straw hat—quirt in hand

"levis" or "blue jeans"—classic working pants—as classic today—in use from the 1850's—made by Levi Strauss—hence the name of levies—indigo-blue denim—orange stitching—copper rivets on strain points—turned up cuffs when too long

angora chaps over levis—cloth vest—linen shirt—gay colored neckerchief—cartridge belt—leather holster—gun—boots—white felt sombrero

RTW

bicycling costume-
blue, brown or
black velvetine-
fitted bolero-
leg-o'-mutton
sleeves-
bloomers-
Ascot scarf-
tam-o'-shanter
of silk
with
plume-
1894

golf and
bicycling
suit of
tweed-
double-breasted
jacket and
knickerbockers-
knit golf hose-
wing collar-
four-in-hand
scarf-
derby-
1895

a
dressy bathing
costume in
navy blue
and white-
alpaca, serge or
bengaline-
combined with
white piqué-coarse,
heavy lace-
fringed sash-
sandals-
"no stockings"-
1896

the
Gibson shirtwaist
girl - starched
white blouse
with Ascot scarf-
dark blue
or black
broadcloth,
"habit-back"
skirt-
pompadour
and
sailor hat-
1899

RTW

CIVIL DRESS
THE 20TH CENTURY

CHAPTER NINE

THE AMERICAN WAY OF LIFE has developed into a true democratic form of living based on culture, work and play. Class distinction, of which we really had little, has been eliminated. Education, the minimum wage law, the possible rise to a high earning power and the disappearance of a servant class has imposed more or less uniformity since World War II. Fashionable clothes were a definite feature of class distinction as worn by the upper class and the wealthy people. But today in our land every man can be fashionably dressed if he wishes since mode and taste can be had in the machine-made piece as in the handmade garment, the difference being in the quality and price. All individuals, on occasions, wear blue jeans, sweaters and sneakers and most families enjoy cars, refrigerators, air-conditioners, radios, television, boats, tennis, golf and travel. No longer can it be said that one can easily distinguish the farmer from the city man by their clothes, speaking not of work clothes but of everyday dress.

The family living far from the city is able to shop out of well-illustrated catalogues which act as salesmen of large mail order houses, a great American institution. Not only clothes but everything for home, farm or wardrobe can be purchased in this manner, a highly successful feature of American living.

MEN—1900 TO 1910

Masculine attire was now of fairly standardized design varying slightly from season to season with London the approved arbiter in such matters. The slim trousers of the 'nineties acquired fullness, young men wearing an exaggerated version called "peg-top" trousers. A wonderful new coat which became a classic was the polo coat of natural color camel's hair which originated in the British "wait coat" thrown over the shoulders between periods of play. The sports costume consisted of the Norfolk jacket, knickerbockers and heavy woolen knitted hose with deep turned-down cuffs. With this went the flat cap of ample béret crown and wide visor. This cap with goggles and the linen duster made up the motoring outfit. Around 1910 the very broad padded shoulders changed to a more natural form without padding which has been the sign of conservative dressing since.

The sports shirt got its start after World War I at the resorts on the Riviera, Bermuda, Florida and California, when fashion-wise men on the alert for comfortable lounge clothes discovered the lightweight, cotton knit shirt of the Basque fisherman of Spain. It became the polo shirt which by the nineteen-twenties appeared without collar for beach wear, bicycle, tennis and golf.

A big change occurred in men's underwear. To the turn of the century, the long union suit of lisle or cotton was the thing for summer, changing to one of wool for winter. The great vogue for sports introduced a new fashion founded upon the athlete's running pants and skeleton shirt. Undergarments became sleeveless lisle shirts and shorts of fine cotton, first white and later in highly colored stripes, plaids and prints. Union suits of lisle, silk or wool, often knee-length, were worn by horsemen.

Until the twentieth century, the only clothes especially designed for sports had been for hunting and riding. As the popularity of sports grew, particularly among college men, appropriate dress was given thought for such games as football, baseball, bicycling, golf and tennis based upon slacks, shirts and knitted shirts.

WOMEN—1900 TO 1910

In feminine dress of the first decade was the high, straight-front corset with long hips, tightly laced in back making the waist as small as possible, a tortuous framework. The curve lessened in 1907, the waist was permitted to spread a bit and the top was cut lower. The new model was equipped with pendant garters replacing the round garter worn for centuries.

In silhouette the skirt continued to be fitted in molded form over the hips and back, flaring out over beflounced petticoats. Dust ruffles faced the under side of the hem which was long enough to sweep the ground, a most un-hygienic fashion. As will happen, the skirt grew shorter and an especially short model in shoe-top length, a "habit-back" of tweed was called a "rainy day skirt" and was only proper when worn on a rainy day.

The rage for the Gibson Girl continued unabated through this decade with her royal carriage, her tiny waist, her beautiful pompadour and her low décol-letage. "Fluffy Ruffles," another dashing beauty, appeared on the scene in 1906 and became a tremendous vogue. She was the creation of the American artist, Wallace Morgan (1873–1948), who made the attractive serial drawings for the New York Herald. She appealed to most young men as the ideal American type and became the model in dress and manners that all women hoped to effect.

In 1905 came the dropped shoulder line, forerunner of the kimono sleeve, an influence of the Russo-Japanese War and a sleeve style that is with us to-day. The silhouette narrowed and straightened into a nineteenth century ver-sion of the First Empire mode. Thus developed the "hobble skirt" which in many instances measured a yard around, necessitating a knee-high slit at the side to make walking possible for the wearer.

The coiffure of the period was the pompadour drawn up high over a pad or roll of false hair called a "rat." Ornamental combs of amber or tortoise shell held the hair in place. By 1908, a New York salon offered permanent waves but not too many women risked the operation until the second decade. The momentous invention occurred in London in 1906, the brain child of Charles Nestlé, a well-known fashionable coiffeur. In the first year only eighteen women were brave enough to endure the eight to twelve hours necessary for the operation or rich enough to afford the fee of one thousand dollars.

Bobbed hair made its appearance on the heads of the Isadora Duncan Dancers shortly before World War I. This was followed in 1913 by the bob of lovely Irene Castle, the photogenic and therefore much photographed ball-room dancer who performed with her husband, Vernon Castle.

Hats were large and perched on top of a pompadour, a bandeau under the crown adding still more height. There was a revival of the large black velvet picture hat trimmed with ostrich, a hat that the eighteenth century portrait painter Gainsborough put on the heads of many of his aristocratic sitters. Also of the first decade was a popular and smart large, black straw sailor or skimmer with low crown known as the Merry Widow after the delightful operetta by the Viennese composer, Franz Lehar.

Motorcar owners were increasing and the open touring car of the day was having an effect upon costume. The unpaved dusty roads made enveloping garments such as the linen duster, automobile bonnets and long chiffon veils an absolute necessity, in fact people soon learned to wear their oldest clothes when motoring out of the city.

The high buttoned and laced shoe of the past half century lasted through this decade, being worn for winter, and Oxfords and slippers in the summer. Day shoes were either black or brown with stockings to match in lisle or silk, silk now becoming less of a rarity. New, and an American fashion, was the feminine adoption of the man's evening pump with the flat, black grosgrain ribbon bow. It appeared about 1904 and was considered startlingly low cut and deshabillé for day or street wear. But it became and still is, the classic piece of footwear after a half century.

By this era the United States had grown into the largest producer of shoes in the world and at the same time the largest consumer of footwear. American shoes are conceded a high position in the realm of fashion and have a definite influence on the European shoe.

Lingerie was embroidered, lace-trimmed and beribboned. Fine handkerchief linen, and sheer, soft batiste, all white, was employed in chemise, drawers and underpetticoat. The chemise was worn under the corset and over the corset went a full-skirted pair of underdrawers and a corset cover. If the bosom were flat, rows of starched narrow frills on the corset cover produced the desired effect, "falsies" being unknown. The Victorian flannel petticoat disappeared but a heavily starched white muslin petticoat was topped by a colored silk one of changeable taffeta.

The bathing suit which dates from the mid-nineteenth century was a non-revealing garment usually of dark blue or black flannel accompanied by self-bloomers and black stockings. The high collar was eliminated and the sleeves were shortened to the elbows.

MEN—1910 to 1920

The greater part of this decade was given over to soldiering and bringing World War I to a successful end for the Allies. Needless to say that any thought given to dress was concentrated upon the uniform. Military costume was bound to affect civilian clothes which it did with an Italian flare, the suit jacket changing to a slim fitted shape, high of waist and a single button closure.

WOMEN—1910 to 1920

Although we are concerned with American everyday dress in this work, from here on American manufacturers were beginning to be conscious of Paris as the fountainhead of new ideas. Magazines and trade papers were really the instigators of this trend and of course, the mercantile trade encouraged what has proven to be big business.

The important events of this decade were the return to the natural figure, the adoption of the simple unadorned frock for day wear and the all-black costume relieved by a piece of jewelry. Paul Poiret was the first couturier daring enough to place the belt directly under the bosom in true Empire style. He made use of the kimono pattern to eliminate the high collar and set-in sleeves. And his palette was of startling combinations in brilliant colors for evening dress. Other new notes were the slim tunic, the lamp-shade tunic and a draped skirt simulating a peg-top silhouette. A divided or trouser skirt, called a harem skirt, met with no success. Lanvin's "robe de style" with a very full skirt, which was considered short because it was eight inches off the ground, became a classic surviving to date.

In 1918 and 1919 the chemise day frock rose to just below the knee, a scant affair with low round neck and sleeveless. For evening it was made with a trailing, panel train. In 1918, Chanel introduced jersey cloth for the chemise and we all have been living in tricot cloth ever since. As far back as 1915 Chanel displayed costumes of American synthetic silk fabrics on her mannequins at the races. The earliest artificial fabrics left much to be desired but they have come a long way, having developed wearing quality and real beauty.

The new figure and the new stance required very little corseting. A soft

160

girdle was designed of knitted elastic tricot, waistline high and just covering the hips. A bandeau or camisole held the breasts flat and the abdomen was thrust forward producing the "boyish form" or the "debutante slouch."

Lingerie became very simple, of sheer batiste or handkerchief linen with just a bit of lace until 1918 when crêpe de chine and silk jersey took over for underwear. Silk became the thing in pink, pale blue and mauve. The petticoat vanished and a silk slim slip was worn under the evening gown if the gown required it, otherwise a bandeau and a pair of silk knickers sufficed under the day frock. And many women from here on wore silk pajamas instead of nightgowns.

The standard black or brown stocking now changed to gray, taupe, Cordovan and tan with gray the most popular. Tan stockings matched spats which were worn with black pumps. White was the stocking color for summer wear. Blond hosiery was an outcome of the dye shortage during the war. French women purchased white stockings and had them dyed beige or blond by a small Paris shop, all this taking place in the second half of the decade. American women clung to long black stockings when bathing although French women, as our soldiers stationed overseas specifically noted, did not wear stockings either with the conventional bathing dress or the one-piece knitted maillot. But new fabrics such as silk jersey and awning-striped colors were adding interest to the American bathing costume.

MEN—1920 TO 1930

The slim, high-waisted silhouette of 1919 was modified into a more conservative style with patch pockets and a two-button closure instead of one. Trousers widened into "Oxford bags" which originated at Cambridge and which were sometimes as wide as twenty-four inches at the bottoms. Knickers grew both in width and length with a deep fall over the golf socks. "Plus fours," as they were called, was the term used by the British Army because breeches were measured as reaching to the knees plus four inches. Breeches of white linen were popular for summer use.

Using synthetic yarns as the base, smart suitings of good woven texture made the summer suit appropriate for city dress in the north as well as in the south where cotton has always been worn during the heated term. The dark business suit gave way to lighter colors and mixtures in all styles and woolen textiles while sports suits were permitted wide liberty in color.

All the classic topcoats continued in fashion. An outstanding American coat of the second and third decades was the huge, bear-like, longed-haired raccoon coat, a favorite in the open touring car and when attending outdoor games in cold weather. There were many other long-haired fur coats but it seems that every college man had to sport a "coonskin coat."

A newcomer in casual hats was the slouch hat of light-weight, paper-thin felt, called handkerchief felt. It was soft yet firm enough to be rolled up and packed in a suitcase.

WOMEN—1920 TO 1930

By 1921 the longer skirt was back having been eased in by long, uneven draping and panels but almost at once the hem crept up to the knees reaching there in 1925. So revealing of feminine charms was the modish creature that she was called a "Flapper" and her period, the "Flapper Age." There was no bosom, no waistline and practically no crowning glory under her tight, skull-shaped felt cloche hat. Wearing her knee-length sheath, she was happy in the thought that she looked like a boy. Within several years the descent of the hem was again in action stopping at ten or twelve inches off the floor for day wear and by 1930, touching the floor for evening dress. Since this occurrence, we have had two distinct hemlines, short for day and long for formal wear.

The boyish form prevailed through this period, the low waistline reaching normal by 1930. The low-cut, knitted elastic girdle, which was boneless as well, aided the desired uncorseted look. And for the first time in corset history that garment was worn next to the skin, the chemise eliminated. A woman's underpinnings consisted of girdle, brassière and panties, or an all-in-one foundation piece which was firmly woven or knitted making a good substitute for the above three. Lingerie was of silk with little or no ornamentation but if lace were used, it was either blond or ecru in color.

New and French was the "ensemble" in soft, dressmaker style, a combination outfit of dress and long coat or skirt and blouse or sweater. From here on sports clothes lost their mannish, tailored look. Of the period was the low-necked, sleeveless sports dress with a scarf or neckerchief tied loosely round the neck. A wardrobe of an ensemble, a basic black day dress and an evening gown filled the needs of almost every occasion.

With the dressmaker type of bathing suit early in the 'thirties long stockings were still to be seen, eventually disappearing. The dress was replaced by the French type of knitted, one-piece swim suit or a combination of knitted maillot or jumper with flannel or knitted shorts of contrasting color.

A radical change in headgear in 1923 was the cloche or mushroom hat of the French milliner, Reboux. A simple round crown with tiny brim and of soft, thin felt, usually black or beige, it was worn summer and winter and enjoyed a long vogue. Relieved by a grosgrain band, or a single jewel, or no trimming at all, it hugged the head tightly down to the eyes in front and to the neck in back. It complimented the bobbed head which was becoming general, to be followed by the shingle in 1922 and next, the wind-blown, shaggy bob. Though many women retained enough hair to dress up, the small head was the smartest.

This decade marks the beginning of the present hey-dey for the manufacture of cosmetics. Every woman, young or old, at leisure or in business, took to the use of "beautifiers" to enhance her looks even if naturally beautiful. The use of powder, lipstick, rouge, eyebrow pencil, eye shadow and foundation cream became general. Repairs were now calmly made in public, a bit of powder or lipstick, without shocking the world. A craze for sun bathing turned many fair complexions to a brown or "sun-tan" coloring in the summer sun or under a sun lamp. Colored nail polish on the fingers of ladies of the Anglo-Saxon world dates from 1926.

MEN—1930 TO 1940

By this time the manufacturers of men's wear were looking with envy at the volume of sales in women's wear and finally consulted the very successful Elsa Schiaparelli who was doing big business in her own American department. She answered that the secret was in seasonal promotion based upon enough change each year to make last year's purchases appear distinctly "last year's." And so, taking the suggestion to heart, the makers of men's wearing apparel have tried to do just that.

The end of the 'twenties brought in "the English drape" in the masculine suit, a one-button single-breasted coat actually fell loosely over the chest. The baggy trousers had pleats at the waist, altogether a dramatic change and good-looking. By 1938 the style had been revised to the English paddock suit with a high-front, two-buttoned closing.

A popular shirt for casual wear was found in California, the "gaucho" having reached there from the Argentine. Made first of flannel, it was developed in silk, cotton and rayon, colors wild or neutral, with tails to be worn outside. By 1935, a cotton version with side slits was the most popular of shirts for beach wear. For cold weather, the fisherman and hunter copied the shirt of the Canadian lumberjack in rich, grayed colors.

Masculine underwear of today consists of skeleton shirt and trunks of cotton cloth, cotton knit and synthetic fabrics. In these days of knitted fabrics enabling one to step in or pull on, buttons have disappeared into limbo. It was in a picture entitled "It Happened One Night" that the late Clark Gable, upon removing his outer shirt, revealed that he "went bare," and since then most young men have been minus an undershirt.

High shoes worn in the early century disappeared. Of tan, brown, gunmetal or patent leather, they were worn fall and winter while low shoes or Oxfords, laced or buttoned, were for summer. The newer sports Oxford acquired a fringed leather tongue covering the lacing, originally intended as protection when tramping over the Scottish moors.

Up to this period American designers of ready-made clothes for men endeavored to create a real American style but with the exception of a few so-called university fashions, the manufacturers concluded that they would rather follow the custom tailors deriving their ideas from London.

Apropos of resort bathing, the American male finally undressed for the sport by wearing just wool or heavy silk swim trunks held secure by an attached, wide elastic belt. When he wished, he covered himself with a beach jacket or lounging robe.

In looking back over this decade one is struck by the wide range of fashions. So specialized did clothes become that there was now a definite costume for each and every occasion—town, country, travel, cocktail parties, the little home dinner party, the formal evening, a design for every sport, even to a sports spectator costume.

We shall note the figure first because both here and abroad the feminine silhouette was influenced by the photoplay of our own Mae West, she of the sumptuous curves. Her great success was the portrayal of a siren of the gay 'nineties in "Diamond Lil." The waistline went back to normal and a slightly boned corset rose higher under the bosom. The bosom again became a feature of the feminine form, being pushed up by a cup-like brassière, and the posture changed from a slouch to a firm position on two feet with chest thrown out and shoulders back.

Propitious indeed were two American inventions of the 'thirties. Lastex was as wonderful a thing as could happen to corsetry. The round elastic core wound or covered with any textile yarn could be woven into a knit fabric. And the slide fastener at last perfected and manufactured in all colors, solved the closure problem. These two items made the corset into a most comfortable silk garment in feel and fit for the first time in its life. The zipper won wide approval as the closure for dress, handbags, household containers, in fact wherever a trim fastening was required.

The halter neck which was designed for bathing dress entered day and evening wear. It was a bib-like bodice drawn up on a cord or ribbon and tied round the neck leaving a back bare to the belt. New and good was the dinner suit usually of black silk in jacket, skirt and blouse based upon the masculine black tie outfit. In 1939, another beach idea was incorporated into evening dress in the "bare midriff," an expanse of bare torso between belt and bolero bodice. Modest females filled in the space with flesh-colored chiffon.

Cotton came back into its own in a big way brought about by publicity campaigns arranged in New York's Madison Avenue. Starting out with white piqué and organza with the aid of synthetics fibers, many new and beautiful weaves have been created which are especially right for summer evening wear. A charming, lasting and youthful fashion and still with us is the Tyrolean dirndl skirt, full and short with tight belt, which got under way when a New

York society woman brought several back from Europe to wear in Southampton and Palm Beach. Of brilliant colors and often hand-worked, the peasant skirt is the perfect answer to many suburban needs of such a casual and attractive garment. It no doubt re-established our shirtwaist dress and also paved the way to Dior's New Look in 1947.

Schiaparelli was responsible for two striking fashions of the 'thirties, one most unflattering to the feminine silhouette. The first was fuchsia pink called "Shocking Pink" and later, Schiaparelli Pink. The other was the broad, squared padded shoulders so disfiguring to the feminine form.

There was just about every style of hat but outstanding examples were the Eugénie hat and the most versatile doll hats, first designed by Talbot for the Duchess of Windsor. Veils were popular and so was every kind of cap or net. From here on, hatlessness became more prevalent than being hatted. Every coiffure or hairdo was modish provided it kept to the small head for which the hair was cut shoulder length, making any headdress possible.

The hatless era of men and women began as early as the late 'twenties, a fashion first seen at the resorts in Southern France and Palm Beach. A whim or a fad, it grew into a real menace to the hat trade and which in these 1960's has not yet been put down. There are several reasons for it, each one of the age in which we live—the expensive hairdo which a woman doesn't wish to disarrange, the closed motor car and lastly, air travel with its restricted luggage weight.

Slipper footwear was of every conceivable design and texture from sandal to pump, the pump predominating. A big change was the replacement of the Louis heel by the high, slim steel spike heel. Except in hot, bare-legged summer weather, the blond stocking still held its own.

The first non-silk stockings were made of wood fiber and proved unsatisfactory. Then came rayon which, combined with lisle or cotton, was a bit more successful in fit. Next, nylon, the finest of synthetic yarns, was woven into gossamer sheer stockings possessing not only fit and beauty but remarkable wearing quality. American nylons came on the market in 1939 but World War II (1939–1945) curtailed the use of nylon yarn for needs vital to the war effort and stockings furnished by the Government went only to those women in its service.

"Fake jewelry" which had always been taboo in good dressing and by the real lady, was first worn without pretense in the 'thirties. From that time, lavish and artistic pieces to complement unadorned costumes have been seriously designed by jewelers and worn by well-dressed women with complete aplomb.

Play clothes were adopted by everyone in the summer regardless of age, size or shape at the resorts, in suburbia and city streets. They included very short dresses resembling children's rompers, slacks and shorts. Underneath might be worn a "pantie girdle" of knitted elastic. The tailored costume of pants and jacket became standard for winter sports especially for skiing. Navy blue or black were the favorite colors in gabardine, whipcord or flannel. For rink ice skating the tailored knee-length dress or shorter, with flaring, circular cut was the most popular costume.

For resort bathing the American woman finally adopted the maillot of the Continent, a one-piece swim suit of knitted or elastic fabric in silk or wool, dark, light or all colors of the rainbow and unusual color combinations.

MEN—1940 TO 1950

The enforced curtailment of civilian manufacturing during the years of World II and the rush to replenish wardrobes upon the soldiers' return home made for the popularity of casual or semi-formal clothes. The influence of battle dress was evident in the passing of the exaggerated square physique which changed to more natural shoulders. A bit of drape was still present in the suit which was either a three-button, single-breasted or a three-button, double-breasted with trousers laid in pressed pleats at the waist. A casualty of the war was the matching vest due to limitations on wool yardage. Patch pockets, pocket flaps and trouser turn-ups were also banned.

War necessities created a dearth in white cotton civilian shirts which were simply unattainable for the man at home. It was in this period that the nylon shirt came upon the scene, a sensation of the 1940's. Its qualities of washability, quick-drying, requiring no pressing or very little, made it seem a practical wonder.

The scarcity of cloth and dyes put men into suits of lighter colors and combinations of colors. Slacks and tweed sports coats became the general tone of dress unless a man's pre-war wardrobe lasted out the period. A smart ensemble for instance, was the jacket of camel's hair cloth with slacks of solid color.

The topcoat of camel's hair held its position and so did the raglan of whipcord. And for a price, a topcoat of vicuña or guanaco could be had and enjoyed by the older non-soldier since the ruling did not effect such luxuries. In the post-war period the returning vets displayed high approval of the well-tailored, lined raincoat. Of light-colored cravenetted cloth it is still a smart and favored coat. Also to be noted is the army coat of water-repellent cotton gabardine, sheepskin lined and collared for real knock-about service.

The popularity of the varied sport model shirts finally suggested a shirt white or colored that would serve as an all-purpose shirt with a convertible collar that could be worn open or closed and with or without scarf.

Scarfs went pretty wild in the late 'forties, no doubt a reaction against the sombre uniform. Many patterns were in brilliant, garish color in silk, wool and synthetic fabrics. But there were also the club and regimental stripes and others of small neat designs, some in solid colors.

The felt hat was most generally worn with a snap brim on the wide side for business and semi-sports. Ribbon bands ranged from narrow to wide in colors rich and muted. The Homburg in dark blue or black with turned-up brim was the elegant shape for dress. Sportsmen revived the wearing of the flat cap.

Myriad have been the straws for summer, hats fashioned of every available South Sea or tropical grass woven in exotic meshes or plain, in Panamas, watersilk palms, coconuts, bakus and many others to combat the hot weather. And mostly all bound with a puggree band of color.

The so-called "loafer shoe" climbed into the staple class. The comfortable, casual Norwegian slipper was eventually tailored for city wear since most men found they liked the ease of the laceless slip-on. A black patent leather model was made to accompany dinner clothes. A smart new style in an ankle-high cut was based upon the boot of polo players and army officers and called the "chukkar" or "flight boot."

Perhaps the biggest story pertaining to costume in the 1940's is that of fabrics. For thousands of years the natural yarns of wool, linen, cotton and silk have been woven into cloth to clothe man. But with the invention of rayon in the last century, the spinning and weaving of the man-made textile filament has come far indeed. By this decade synthetic yarn production in the United States exceeded that of the world with Japan following in second place.

Since the last war, out of the laboratories seem to flow an ever-increasing number of synthetic fibers which go into fabrics for garments for male and female. The new test-tube yarns have remarkable properties such as lowered cost, can be submitted to washing and drycleaning, furnish insulation against heat and cold and are light in weight. Furthermore miracles in fashion are evolved by blending the artificial fibers with natural ones, thereby utilizing the good qualities of both.

Perhaps even more remarkable is the new, stretchable synthetic yarn of which is fashioned all manner of form-fitting garments for men, women and children. One such elastic piece will fit many sizes and different shapes thus eliminating the need of so many sizes in a given model. And stretchables give the luxurious feel of fitting perfectly.

But wonderful as the new fabrics are, wool, linen and silk continue to hold their own except in women's stockings. In that category, nylon because possessed of amazing textile strength no matter how sheer has surpassed and supplanted natural silk.

The trend of the 'thirties toward a smaller waist, diaphragm control and a rounded bosom stood still during the war years until Paris again hit her stride in fashion and produced the "New Look" in 1947. After nearly half a century of the pencil-slim form Madame came forth equipped with bosom, hips, stomach and derrière, all this womanly allure the result of new corsetry. Needless to say it delighted the picture makers of Hollywood. There appeared an effective little girdle which rose not more than a few inches above the waist and covered about the same space below, this the "waist cincher." To-day's use of nylon, elastic and power net gives a woman a form-shaping garment that she is more comfortable with than without.

In 1947 while fashion was still in the doldrums, a new Paris couturier, Christian Dior (1905–1957), a former successful art dealer, turned his creative talents to women's clothes and presented the feminine world with a silhouette that came to be known as the "New Look." It was an instant and tremendous success because not only did women like it but it proved to be the way that most men liked to see their women look. Rounded bosom, small waist and full skirt, all making for flattery and charm. And of course, it was just what was needed to prod the needlework trades.

Full skirts called for petticoats, even crinolines and several underskirts worn together—"petticoat fever," it was called. In colored taffeta heavily flounced, and crinoline stiffened with horsehair and featherboning, organdie and white cotton beruffled with narrow frills, embroidery and lace, all made a return appearance reviving the obsolete underskirt manufacture.

This very feminine fashion was the inspiration for an American idea of mother and daughter dresses that met with success in a costume design made identically the same for the young mother and her little daughter.

White, pale pastels and "flesh rose" were the prevailing lingerie colors but deep hues in violet, rose and mimosa yellow also built up quite a following. Especially new and chic was black faille for the black day dress and dinner gown, and usually corset, bras and panties matched.

A pleasant post-war custom has been the cocktail hour, calling for a short evening or dinner dress for home or restaurant from five o'clock on. The American couturier Valentina in the early 'forties created the "ballerina length" as she termed it, fulfilling a need for the dressy but not formal look when a woman's escort is in his business suit.

Fascinating little hats ranging from pillboxes, turbans, bérets and bowknots to large hats were worn principally in the city streets while the hatless creature continued on her merry way.

The shoes of the peoples down the ages gave inspiration to modern footwear, shoe designers creating such pieces as simple or extravagant as any woman might wish. The resulting styles ranged from moccasin and sandal to the slim, steel spike heel and baby French heeled pump.

The most abbreviated of bathing attire finally reached our shores in the "bikini" from the French Riviera. It put in an appearance in 1947 and 1948 with a few inches added to the French original. As a style it was fleeting, in fact, the bikini, consisting of a narrow bra and a narrow G-string, appears to have created a trend toward a more covered-up look. New models were developed with long tight sleeves and low back. Many were made with a built-in bra, others with an all-in-one foundation especially in the knitted maillot model. And many were planned with a wrap-around skirt for dining at the beach club or restaurant.

MEN—1950 TO 1960

The 1950's can really go down as the gray and black period in masculine suit history. The gray flannel suit was in charcoal bloom at the beginning of the decade especially among the Ivy League university crowd. Then it was reported that black sports clothes were sighted on the Riviera, next in California and the East, followed by a news items of 1952 that black was being worn in London and that did it! From then on all suit cloth seemed to turn black or "tawny black" with colored specks or stripes, all of which lasted here in America just about a decade.

There has been enough sartorial change in men's wear in this period to suggest that the manufacturers' campaign to get the male into something new each season or yearly has borne fruit. The draped suit with wide lapels passed away being replaced by a slimmer, natural silhouette, an influence of the Ivy League look. Slim trousers, natural shoulders and narrow lapels on a straight, unshaped coat without padding have been the marks of the so-called Ivy League suit based upon the traditional, conservative elegance of Bond Street. It has been worn throughout the century by some Yale, Harvard and Princeton men.

The Ivy stronghold is now being besieged by the Continental look, an American version of the above Edwardian style. A two-button jacket is slightly shorter than the Ivy with a slight waist suppression and a more rounded cutaway front. Breast pockets and lapel buttonholes were eliminated in the first models but quickly replaced when the absence of these features was found to be a drawback to the future of the design. The matching vest is again being supplied by manufacturers.

Color has again come into the picture with the increasing use of patterned cloths in glen plaids, herringbone tweeds and worsteds in heather mixtures of blues, the new golds and olives along with grape or plum hues.

In the past few years the men's wear market has been flooded with cloths made of synthetic fibers, namely wool and cotton plus some linen and silk.

The first objective of the makers is to produce a wrinkle-proof cloth and the second consideration is the washable, drip-dry advantage. Some are wool-like in texture, others resemble linen or silk. There are at least a half dozen well-known names advertised, and under a recent law every garment must be tagged with a label listing its principal fibers. Traditional seersucker also becomes wash-and-wear with the blending of synthetic yarn.

In line with the general trend towards lighter-weight clothing one hears less of overcoats and greatcoats than of topcoats. Topcoats are not so formal, are shorter and sportier. Strong patterns appear in the cloth of the short coat, also camel's hair, fine gabardines, coverts and rough textured tweeds. For suburban wear and bad weather in town there are pile fabrics of man-made or pure wool fibers, deep and rich, knitted and woven. Pile fabrics are also made into double-breasted ulsters, short "British Warms" and finger-tip length coats with leather trimming. Colors run to nutria, beaver and black.

The well-styled wash and drip-dry raincoat is one of the most successful newcomers. The conservative town version is very often used the year round by some business men and is also a great traveler. White and black are newer and exceedingly smart but natural and beige are the prevalent colors.

Jackets and sweaters for winter or summer in white and in synthetic fabrics have appealed to men. Very light in weight, they are no longer impracticable because easy to clean by washing and are also spot-resistant.

Evening wear has reached an informal stage, dinner jackets having usurped the natural easy lines of the business suit. Because of central heating and closed cars heavy fabrics have given way to tropical worsteds, man-made fibers blended with wool and winter-weight silks. The charcoal gray dinner jacket with dull, black satin shawl collar was a new note in 1954. For less formal wear after dark, good-looking jackets are made of multi-colored cotton batik prints, all in toned-down colors.

Quite a few new fashions have been set by the college man, some like the raccoon of the earlier years were pure college fads. Some, like the Norwegian loafer, spread to the outside world and into the business office. From the campus came the smart combination of sports jacket and gray slacks.

Shorts and slacks share honors for casual wear, golf, beach or whatever, according to season. Bermuda shorts, those impeccably tailored breeches, made news on the streets of New York City in the summer of 1953. And quite a few brave young men attended country club dances in shorts with dinner jackets.

The white shirt is still the classic shirt but color was rampant in this decade so that even pink became permissible in the office. Probably the run on colored shirts can be laid to the popularity of the gray and charcoal gray suit. Another shirt which has appeared in the office these several past hot summers is the short-sleeved shirt in cool weaves and open meshes. Of the 1960's are combination sports shirts and shorts printed with dazzling, colorful motifs from South America, the Far East and India.

The hatless male by 1950 had become as much a problem as the female of the species to hatmakers so that they banded together in an attempt to improve their lot. Like women, men did occasionally buy a hat but did not wear it. The fedora was re-designed with narrow brim and a lowered tapered crown which met with some success but not too much. In the next move, felts and straws were given flat-topped crowns. More casual felts and fancy straws were banded with silk, cord or braid in deep, rich color and some further dressed up with Tyrolean feather ornaments. The biggest change was in the narrowed brim, which as far as looks go, was not a change for the better. This being a study of everyday dress we shall pass by the elegant derby, the Homburg and the top hat.

Sports hats were re-styled in suède, velours, tweed and other rough mixtures. By 1956, the hatmaker displayed no qualms in attacking the traditional southern and western ten-gallon hat and giving it too a flat-top crown and narrowed brim. In 1958 one finds crushable summer straws available in panama, tissue Milan, split macora, raffia, with even the boater made softer and with snap brim. The peaked flat cap is very much in style and developed in new shapes adding dash to men's dress in plaids, tweeds and colorful cloth or cotton.

As to neckwear, scarfs too have narrowed and in pattern are as subdued, monotone or brilliant as the wearer might wish.

The shoe story of the last decade fits in here with design continuing to stress the leather rising to the ankles and tapered toe, especially in the Norwegian loafer and chukkar models. As to color, olive tones are replacing the former blacks and browns.

Up into the twentieth century, everyday dress in an everyday family usually meant that last year's best became this year's everyday wear while a new piece was acquired for "Sunday best." For the woman who did her own housework, there has always been the simple, inexpensive cotton dress of calico or gingham. It was the "at home costume" on the farm or in the suburbs until the nineteen thirties when slacks and shorts became popular for sports. And then, as the hired girl disappeared, slacks and shorts took the place of the cotton frock. When, during the 'thirties college students of the University of California began wearing blue denim pants or "levis," blue jeans appeared on every campus in the country and at home.

Little did Levi Strauss think that his well-made work pants would ever grow into a country-wide fad but they did! Blue jeans which had been the western cowboy's leg covering for nearly a century were adopted by the feminine world as well. When Levi Strauss went to California in 1850 as a gold prospector he prudently decided to make work pants of indigo blue denim re-inforced with copper rivets at crucial points. He supplied a garment so desperately needed that he made his fortune doing just that, instead of panning for gold. And he also became famous for his product which hence-forth was called "levis."

In golf and tennis the former suit and dress have been replaced by Bermuda shorts and the newer above-knee-length termed Jamaica shorts which are worn with the kilt. Golf shorts may be of woolen cloth or cotton according to season but the tennis outfit is invariably white and definitely without frills.

Ever since the turn of the century, the shirtwaist dress, or by its modern name the shirtdress, has been more or less a perennial American style in a woman's wardrobe. Sheath, Empire or dropped waistline may come and go but the shirtdress is ever with us. And the peasant dirndl skirt, as a separate, still fits well into American everyday dress in cotton, silk or wool and hem line high or low.

The controversial chemise or "sack" which appeared in 1954 originated in Vogue Magazine which pictured a striped-round sports shirt knitted to dress length. Though it drew upon itself the most scathing criticism, it has survived as a smart, comfortable and easily packed garment in all fabrics.

The tailored suit of the decade has been a youthful, straight and short jacket with simple skirt which was a pet Chanel creation of the 'twenties. After an absence of fifteen years she returned to the haute couture in 1954 bringing back her little suit accented by matching blouse and lining of a brilliant silk print. The revival proved a huge success!

A sensation of the 1960's was the tailored town suit introduced by the American designer Norman Norell. Culottes which give the effect of a slightly flaring skirt are a skillfully-cut trouser skirt worn with pull-over or blouse and jacket. The cleverly concealed division is a real solution for the wearer when climbing in and out of the present low cars, in fact when active anywhere in public. The knee-length skirts necessitating such a solution came into vogue in 1957.

"Frankly fake furs" became fashion news around 1950. Designed primarily with the college girl in mind, the manufacturer has so improved his product to the point that designers are successfully using the synthetic fur cloths in sophisticated short jackets and handsome greatcoats. An insulated lining makes the garment as cozy and protective as the real pelt and at a tremendous saving. The imitations are available in Persian lamb, broadtail, moleskin, beaver, sealskin, krimmer and other short-haired furs.

As to hats they are fashioned in all shapes, fabrics, furs and straws, large of crown and as small as one might desire. And though hat-wearing has risen steadily of late, many hatless ones are still to be noted about town.

A novelty of the 1950's was the dress-up sweater created by the American-French couturier Mainbocher who returned home to New York after World War II. He revamped knitted sweaters into fairy-like little jackets, chiffon lined and sparkling with paillettes, beads, braid and ribbon embroidery. Society women wore them in Palm Beach, Long Island and European resorts.

The coiffure of the 1950's was predominately bouffant, cut short with but slight wave. Both chrysanthemum and artichoke are words descriptive of the shape. As of 1961, the head is becoming more soigné and reminiscent of the 'twenties, a rather trim cut with hair curling over forehead and cheek. As to color any women may have any color she wishes, she may even change it, say once a month and no one is surprised or wonders. She can have it done at the beauty parlor or may do it at home successfully. There are many safe coloring kits on the market under the headings of rinse, tint, bleach or dye which can be combed in, brushed or washed in, the color being permanent, or lasting only to the next shampoo.

An important part of everyday dress is the use of make-up which from the commercial angle has become big business. Taboo a half century ago, every woman today from highschool girl to grandmother at least applies a coating of lipstick as essential to her dressing for the day. Most women are artists in achieving a natural effect with cosmetics, except for some lipsticks and nail enamels which occasionally are arbitrary colors applied for accent. The use of cosmetics is no longer a deep secret but simply a matter of grooming and most men expect their women to avail themselves of beauty aids. The visit to the beauty salon at least once a week is every woman's custom in America.

Twentieth Century
1900-1910

gown of tucked
linen and
lace-velvet
ribbon belt-
straw hat
with roses-
1900

single-breasted
sack suit-
gray cloth
with fine stripe-
pearl gray
fedora-bow
tie-black
shoes-
1905

short top coat
of reddish
brown cloth-
striped brown
trousers-
brown derby-
black
shoes-
1907

"Fluffy Ruffles,"
a stylish American miss
created by
Wallace Morgan-
dark blue
tailored suit-
white shirtwaist-
hat with
fluffy feathers-
black pumps-
white silk
stockings-
1906

RTW

black and white Scotch tweed-white linen shirtwaist-Ascot tie-fringed yellow cashmere scarf-tan leather gauntlets-black silk sailor hat-white silk stockings-tan and brown shoes-1919

aviation outfit of leather-lined with camel's hair-smock-breeches-puttees over shoes-gauntlets-cap-1910

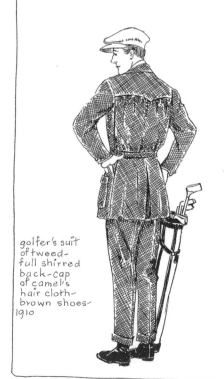

golfer's suit of tweed-full shirred back-cap of camel's hair cloth-brown shoes-1910

black and white for tennis-"permissible in that season", says the reporter of dress news-1915

the "little black dress" of crêpe de chine- pleated flounces- black felt cloche with grosgrain ribbon band- beige suede "slip-ons"- blond stockings- black sandals- 1926

golf suit of tweed with "plus four" breeches- sport shirt- four-in-hand scarf- panama hat white buckskin shoes- plaid woolen hose- 1928

the raccoon or "coonskin" coat- beloved of the college man- "Oxford bag" trousers- slouch hat of "handkerchief" felt- 1925

the "ensemble" of the period- black cloth coat and skirt- beige astrakan lining- beige crêpe de chine blouse with ascot tie- front pleats in skirt- black felt cloche- leather envelope bag- 1929

RTW

women took
to slacks and
shorts-
occasionally
a complete
suit-dark
blue woolen
cloth-blue
béret-white
shirt and
Ascot tie-
white buckskin
shoes

golf and
country
wear-shirt of
wine color
basket weave
cotton-
brilliant
silk muffler-
beige flannel
slacks with
pleats at
waist-tan
suède
shoes

polo coat-
natural
color
camel's hair-
cloth-horn
buttons-
self belt
with leather
buckle-
brown slouch
hat- brown
calf shoes

dirndl skirt-
Guatemalan
hand-loomed
charcoal gray
linen with
multi-colored
border-white
cotton
shirtwaist-
brilliant
silk
headkerchief

RTW

Dior's "New Look" of 1947-curves and tiny waist-black cloth and accordion pleated dark green taffeta-black suède belt-green velvet béret-black pompon-black suède pumps

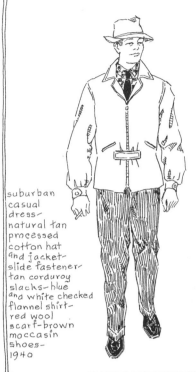

suburban casual dress-natural tan processed cotton hat and jacket-slide fastener-tan corduroy slacks-blue and white checked flannel shirt-red wool scarf-brown moccasin shoes-1940

western leisure dress founded upon the Spanish charro (cowboy) style-blue denim levies and jacket-slide fastener-checked shirt-abbreviated scarf-black felt sombrero-boots-1948

costume for after ski wear-black velveteen slacks with velvet fringe-steel studded suède belt-tucked white blouse-colored chiffon scarf-suède slippers-1947

RTW

the
controversial
shift, chemise or
sacque of silk,
wool, cotton or
synthetic fabric-
bouffant
coiffure-
blond gloves
and stockings-
black pumps-
1955

suit of
raspberry
pink wool
tweed-
black velvet
tutulus
bonnet-
black suède
pumps-
1956

the change in the
masculine silhouette
from 1950 to 1960-
narrow shoulders,
jacket and trousers-
return of the vest-
narrow scarf-
trimmed-down slouch
hat- slim, tapered
high-rise shoes

RTW

CHILDREN
16TH — 20TH CENTURIES
CHAPTER TEN

16TH AND 17TH CENTURIES

IN THE PORTRAITS OF CHILDREN of earlier centuries the tiny figures in their rich dress-up clothes look like dwarf adults. And adults were what their elders were trying to make of them, not only in appearance but mentally too. In the homes of European upper classes, infants were often put to study under tutors and governesses when about three years old. From contemporary letters and diaries, one learns that education was concentrated upon so early that it was not unusual for a child of four or five to be able to read, write and understand as well as to speak several languages.

Dressing children in adult style came about in the Renaissance with the increase of wealthy merchant families, especially in the cities. Thus developed a love of finery that in earlier times had been accessible only to nobility. And since costly clothes have ever been the outward sign of affluence, it was important that the children be as richly dressed as their parents. However, indoors "en famille" the garb consisted of a coarse, unbleached linen chemise or smock which was the undergarment worn under the handsome dress.

This undergarment whether of linen or woolen cloth was the sole piece of underwear worn by men, women and children of both sexes. As the general body garment for babies, it came to be known in the thirteenth century as the "gertrude," the name still in use today for the flannel petticoat of the new baby. Research reveals that a Saint Gertrude of German birth was "Gertrude the Great," an abbess of Nivelle in Brabant who lived from 1256 to 1311. She was famed for having received supernatural visions but certainly, too, must always have worn a woolen piece of underwear.

183

Dress-up clothes were for occasions of entertaining and visiting and like those of the adults, were of satin, velvet, brocade and occasionally of white satin worked with gold and silver thread. Since the heavy fabrics were reinforced with buckram glued to the under side, underwear was of little consideration except as a protection for the gown in touching the body.

The coif or bonnet of linen was always worn during the Middle Ages indoors and out because it was considered wise to keep the head of a child covered, a thought that applied to adults as well, the coif being worn for centuries.

Little boys wore the incongruous busk-front doublet and little girls were dressed in the stiff stomacher of the period. There were the same dark colors, principally green and brown, and the same hard, board-like corset underneath. Corsets in those days were of heavy, boned canvas or of "cuir bouilli" which was boiled leather.

A custom which lasted into the eighteenth century in Europe and the Colonies was that of dressing little tots, both boy and girl in the same ankle-length dress. Boys wore the dress to five or seven years when they were "breeched." It is amazing to find when studying the contemporary portraits of children that one cannot tell boy from girl except by name. Over the elaborate frock as protection was worn a "pinafore," an apron pinned to the front, often of sheer linen, embroidered and lace-trimmed.

Swaddling clothes or "bands" were what babies were bound up in, the new baby encased in a sort of pocket with board back, of quilted cotton cloth ornamented with frills and elaborately embroidered. The child's hands and feet were held in place and the ears held close to the head by its cap. The contraption resembled the American Indian's packsack for carrying around the papoose. One could carry the child on one's back, could place it on its back in the cradle or hang it on the wall.

A fashion of the days when fashions lasted for a hundred years or more was "hanging sleeves." An extra pair of sleeves often slashed, hung unused in back as a purely ornamental feature of the rich costume of man, woman or child. A mode of the Renaissance, it carried over into the seventeenth century, worn in Europe and in the Colonies. Hanging sleeves were seen longer in children's dress especially on the very young. After it passed, one would come upon the expression in literature of the eighteenth century, "hanging sleeves" being applied to an infant or an elderly person signifying either childhood or second childhood.

In Europe, England and America there developed a tendency to brighten youngsters' clothes with touches of scarlet, a color which took hold among the subdued Quakers. It became a favorite accent especially in linings that revealed themselves as in capes and sleeves and in ribbon bowknots and tassels.

CHILDREN—THE 18TH CENTURY

It was in England in the first quarter of the century when someone had the inspiration that boys should wear sailors' trousers. English seamen had been dressing in pantaloons since the seventeenth century and English boys adopted trousers a half century before their fathers did. English children were the first to be emancipated, little girls changing to soft, unlined frocks in the 1770's with France and the Colonies following next.

Some well-known writers had taken the age to task for its manner of confining infants' bodies in tight clothes, among them John Locke, the English philosopher (1632–1704), who was probably the big influence in the change. He was followed by Jean Jacques Rousseau, the French philosopher (1712–1775), who carried on the crusade and was forced to flee Paris for England because of his revolutionary ideas.

Although the change over to trousers occurred early in the period, knee breeches were still worn for dress as can be seen in contemporary portraits. The writings of the Age of Reason were having an effect in putting children into comfortable clothes, the trouser costume known as the English sailor's dress being a short little jacket over an open-necked blouse, a waistcoat without skirts and the long breeches.

The little girl's frock was usually a sheath of muslin with round neck and short or long sleeves. From the 'seventies on, the floor-length skirt slowly shortened to the ankles revealing the soft little slippers of kid or fabric instead of the earlier, heavy buckled shoes.

Infants' swaddling clothes lasted well into the eighteenth century. The baby also owned a complete set of dress clothes which were worn for the christening ceremony and any other public occasion. Such garments were exquisitely made and beautifully embroidered. The skirts attached to the tiny bodices were invariably a good four feet in length. Yellow was the traditional color for the christening dress with embroidery in silk, or gold for an "upper class baby."

CHILDREN—THE 19TH CENTURY

The first two decades of this era were the period in which the Empire fashion raised waistlines of mother, daughter and small boy up under the arms. This basically classic style regardless of the age in which it returns is always charming and artistic. It is the most appropriate of all children's costumes ever designed, especially for little girls. And so must have thought Kate Greenaway (1846–1901) when she chose that particular period for her lovely illustrations which we shall note in the 1880's.

Playclothes were made of muslin and nankeen. With their long pantaloons, boys wore short jackets, a soft blouse and a round-brimmed hat with a ribbon band. During the wig period of the preceding century it was not unusual to dress a boy's hair like a wig and dust it with powder. Now the hair was cropped instead of the former tortuous curl-papers, curling iron and pomade. Little girls were freed of the boned, corset body, wearing instead a soft muslin dress sash-bound in place of lined silks and velvets.

A slip was worn under the slim frock and as the style shortened, frilled, lace-trimmed tubes or "false pantalets" tied at the knees were designed as modesty pieces to conceal the legs. Occasionally noted in the new fashion journals that had come into existence, such illustrations shocked many to see legs featured in this manner. Seemingly, folks grew accustomed to the fact that females do have legs because by the 1830's, both young girls and women did wear drawers. But it required a quarter century for the garment to become custom in feminine dress. In America the fashion prevailed from 1818 to 1858, that is the fashion of pantalets showing below the skirts. From a contemporary fashion note we learn that pantalets for day wear were of nankeen or calico and that those worn during a period of mourning were of black crêpe.

Here in America during the first quarter of the century caps were still worn in the house and outdoors by children and women. Upon going out, a hat or bonnet of straw or beaver, according to the season, was put on over the cap and tied under the chin, a very becoming fashion to all females.

The cloak was called a "wrapping cloak" which had a cape collar. When trimmed or lined with fur it was a pelisse. Usually of scarlet cloth when intended as a winter wrap, it was wadded and lined and often edged with a narrow strip of fur. Infants were wrapped in long cloaks of merino, painstakingly and lovingly embroidered, wadded and lined with soft silk and edged with swansdown, a baby's garment for most of the century.

In the 'twenties the waistline went back to normal, skirts grew fuller and puffed sleeves appeared in the leg-o'-mutton style. Fashion swung from the simplicity of the earlier mode to as much ruffling, ribbon, ruching, embroidery and trimming as the garment would hold. Hats and bonnets were decked with all the bowknots they could carry. The dainty white and tinted muslins, lawns, percales and gauzes gave way to organdie, gingham and taffeta in deeper colors. From here on into the first decade of the twentieth century design in costumes was doomed to clutter and fussiness.

Another garment was added to the small boy's wardrobe in a knee-length tunic or smock, belted at the waist. This was the costume in all-white linen or merino that American boys were put into when "breeched," an event which usually took place about the age of four. Boys' sleeves were as diversified in shape as were their sisters', slim, full and leg-o'-mutton. They wore caps and hats like their fathers', even to the topper. The suit of older boys comprising trousers, short jackets, waistcoat and white shirt with lay-down collar was known to Americans as the "Eton" because worn in Eton College, England, since that time.

During the Romantic Period in the 1830's there was quite a flare for dressing boys in historical costume, especially in Europe. They were garbed in doublets, hussar tunics, Spanish dress, the Van Dyck style and Turkish too. The trend in America was for the Scottish kilt and the sailor suit, both an influence of Queen Victoria's love for Balmoral Castle and the baby Prince of Wales.

All legs whether of boy or girl were covered to the ankles by trousers, pantaloons which were those fulled or shirred at the ankles, and pantalets. Another feature of the 1830's was the apron for little girls. One reads that those of fine white muslin, white cross-barred cambric and printed calico were not as fashionable as aprons of silk, green in color and made with brettelles, the whole edged with self-ruching.

The crinoline ranges between 1840 and 1865 and was the silhouette of the period for all females large and small. Like that of the grown-ups, the crinoline of the 'forties was a full petticoat corded and stiffened with crin, the French word for horsehair braid. The crinoline was also bolstered by several starched skirts over one of flannel. In the 'fifties came the petticoat of wire hoops held together by tapes, an American invention called the American cage in Europe. It was very light in weight and a wonderful relief after the wearing of such a clutter of muslin underskirts. By the 'sixties the skirt fullness was being pushed toward the back in the trend to the bustle of the 'seventies.

Regardless of full skirts, pantalets were still in the picture but very often they had turned into long frilled drawers. Stockings striped round the legs in bright colors came into vogue for boys and girls. Shoes for both were the flat-soled strap slipper, while for outdoors an ankle-high shoe with elastic sides was proper and popular.

For young ladies not blessed with curls, round combs and ribbon snoods kept the beautifully brushed hair in place. Long hair in those days was every woman's desire yet some girls wore their hair cropped like their brothers'. The Madonna center part was copied from Queen Victoria's headdress, a fashion of several decades. Bangs came into the mode with bonnets continuing to frame the Victorian faces.

In the 'seventies and the early 'eighties, the mode of the Basque bodice of grown-ups appeared in girls' dress as well, a long waist encircled by a wide, crushed sash. The ruffled skirts were bunched up in back giving a panier or bustle effect. The English name for the period was "tied-back time." In the 'seventies girls wore either black or russet leather button shoes usually with long white stockings. In the 'eighties the black or brown shoes were accompanied by stockings to match.

Small boys went from petticoats into "short pants" cut off above the knee but sometimes wore kilt-pleated skirts until about six years old. While in skirts, it was not unusual for boys to wear hanging curls and perhaps bangs but the curls were cut when the boy was breeched, an occasion which brought tears to the eyes of many a doting mother. The young men wore black or rust laced shoes but with black ribbed stockings.

A baby's trousseau or layette of the nineteenth century was composed of a robe, muslin petticoat, woolen undershirt, underwaist and woolen body band. The English term for cap or bonnet was "biggin," the name of the cap worn by the nuns of the Dutch religious society of the Beguines which the modern baby cap resembled. The cap was of cambric or wool. Cloak and dress skirts were easily four feet long, everything lace-edged and covered with fine hand embroidery. The color of the christening robe was now pale blue for boys and pale pink for girls.

In 1886 appeared the book "Little Lord Fauntleroy" written by the English-American novelist, Mrs. Frances Hodgson Burnett (1849–1924). The book was responsible for an enduring vogue of boy's clothes in the style of the Cavalier or Van Dyck Period worn by the young hero of the story. The pictures were the creation of Reginald Birch, the artist who illustrated the story, and many an American youngster secretly hated him for being compelled to wear the black velvet suit with deep lace collar and red or black satin sash, long hair and a picturesque plumed hat.

As mentioned earlier, it was in the 1880's that Kate Greenaway's charming drawings of children met with tremendous success. In her little birthday books and cards which were first published in 1873 she adapted the Empire style to her own taste producing little figures that appealed to everyone. The costumes were simple, artistic designs that were more suitable to little tots than the current over-decorated mode. She became famous in Europe and America and her little boys and girls have come down to us in the dress of the small pages and flower bearers in wedding pageants.

The sailor suit was a fashion of the end of the century for both boys and girls. Boys wore the tunic with long pantaloons while girls wore the tunic with the kilted skirt. The suits were made in blue or white serge for winter and of French flannel, linen or duck for summer.

The apron or pinafore continued as part of girl's dress, worn at home, in school and at play, and a very special one, sheer with lace and embroidery for dressy afternoon affairs. Girls were not supposedly adult until they reached eighteen, which meant that the waist-cinching, back-laced corset was not put on until that age. Hair was dressed hanging until seventeen or eighteen, then turned up at the nape or thereabout. Skirts were the real telltale of the age, just below knee-length at twelve, calf-length at fourteen, to the ankle at sixteen and full-length when the hair was dressed high on the head.

1900 to 1920. With the new century came a change in the trousseau or layette of the new baby, at least in the length of dress, coat and petticoats. Quite a piece was cut off the garments, the new length of twenty-seven inches from neck to hem seemingly short indeed. In some cases where a long robe is used it is because the christening robe is a family heirloom. But babies are no longer swaddled as they formerly were, sometimes living almost bare the first summer of their lives, a fact that would have made our forebears shudder. And it all began with play "rompers."

Children's dress was now specifically designed for children and did not hold to any one pattern. At least clothes were simple and childlike. The small girl's dress covered her knees and her waistline was placed low. Tots under six wore a baby style, soft, full frocks shirred to a tiny yoke. Though schoolgirls wore shirtwaist and skirt there were three popular and almost uniform styles for that age and under, the sailor costume or "middy" blouse, the Russian tunic with pleated skirt and the jumper dress of navy serge worn over a lingerie blouse or "guimpe." Accordion pleating designated a party dress.

From about 1908 for everyday wear small girls for play wore bloomers instead of drawers and petticoats. The legs of American children were still encased in long stockings although socks were coming in and being covered by leggings in winter. Cold weather always called for high, buttoned or laced shoes and in summer, Oxfords and strap shoes.

As to hats, the older miss wore youthful versions of grown-up fashions, securing the hat to the hair by means of a long, vicious looking hatpin instead of the chin-elastic of childhood.

It was in the hairdo that teen-agers went fancy free. With either center or side part most young females wore long curls, flowing hair or long braids or dressed the front hair into a pompadour and tied it with a bowknot. And, on the subject of bowknots, wide ribbon was the thing and often not just one bowknot but two big bows. All this was followed by the Dutch cut with straight, trimmed bangs.

Like their sisters boys also dressed in sailor suits and the Russian blouse. A suit resembling the Russian blouse was the American Buster Brown tunic with wide starched collar and black silk scarf. Buster Brown was a popular, small hero of a Sunday newspaper serial which had quite a following among the youngsters. The older boys wore knee pants with tunic or short jacket and about 1910, one notes the Norfolk jacket with knickers and white shirt. Collar and tie accompanied the Norfolk outfit. It was custom for American boys to adopt trousers in their teens. During the first decade long, ribbed, black stockings were worn with high, laced, black shoes, or Oxfords according to season. And on the head, sailor caps or flat caps with peaks.

1920 to 1930. The knitting fever of the war years carried over into civilian life of the 'twenties but in soft yarns of lovely colors, in sweaters and caps. Children's clothes were now designed with knee length skirts and knee shorts, both garments growing shorter and shorter. Boys took to wearing flannel, tweed and serge suits with shirts and scarfs like those of their elders, topped by the béret and also the peaked cloth cap. Girls' dresses were of gay fabrics with flowered, striped and spotted motif. Most little girls wore their hair short and boys had their heads cropped. Small misses wore the béret, the cloche and soft tams. And all had adopted short socks, including the younger teen-agers, whence the name of "bobby-soxers."

1930 to 1940. Little folks' clothes seemed quite perfect in the 'thirties, tailored and so simple in line. Dresses were short and so were a young man's breeches. Girls of all ages wore the classic Chanel suit while boys had a choice of the older style business suit, the Norfolk with knickers and if he were inclined to be dressy, the English Eton suit of short jacket, vest (when of self-fabric), trousers and a derby, if you please! Under the smart little coats girls wore party dresses of crêpe georgette, voile or crêpe de chine exquisitely hand-worked with tiny tucks, smocking, piping and fine pleating yet retaining the over-all simple effect. Youngsters now had quite a wardrobe of play or sports clothes ranging from basic rompers, sun suits to snow suits.

1940 to 1960. There are still dress-up clothes in the youthful wardrobe but lots more exciting are the school and sports outfits. Young people now live in an age calling for simple, casual tailored garments, smart-looking yet thoroughly comfortable and really fun-clothes. Such dress has settled into a pattern.

For both sexes there are principally sweaters, pull-ons, all kinds of knock-about jackets, shorts, slacks and for girls, the attractive dirndl skirts, and all kinds of outer coats of varied length practical for sports and school wear. In tailored suits it is the Chanel model for girls and the rough tweed for boys. And the raincoat which is no longer what a raincoat used to be. Extremely smart-looking, it is more utilitarian than ever, serving as a all-around coat of water-repellent cotton or wool with removable linings that button, snap or zip in or out according to the needs of the weather. Winter coats are lined with thick, fuzzy synthetic pile that feels and looks like fur. And there are blue jeans or levis for roughing it and accessories too numerous to itemize.

There is a current vogue for a gay, youthful negligee, new in 1957 or 1958, called a Muu-Muu. It was first worn in a mid-western college by a young female student who had been to Hawaii. It is a hot climate version of the cotton house wrapper American women wore at home in the nineteenth century. Missionaries carried these house robes of calico and gingham out to Hawaii to clothe the naked pagans who liked the bright-colored cottons but cut neck and cut off the sleeves for comfort. And so, in that fashion the Mother Hubbard of the westerners has come full circle as the Muu-Muu.

From North Bay, Ontario in the 1950's came word that young mothers have discovered with surprise and great pleasure the wonderful convenience of the cradleboard used by the Indian mothers for centuries. It seems that the campers are making use of the "tikanagum" to transport the baby when walking over the rough ground, wearing the contraption on their backs. They have found it perfect for car use too, the little passenger evidently enjoying riding in a mobile cradle. The packsack is pure American, being made by local Indian women. No nails are used, all wooden parts tied together with leather thongs and the whole gadget ornamented with lace and beads, a true piece of Americana in origin and age.

Sixteenth Century

embroidered linen coif and apron- beige frock- red sleeves with embroidered motif- green and beige embroidery on skirt- green cloth stockings- red slippers- Italian- late 15th C.

boy in scarlet frock- hanging sleeves- gold braid and buttons- white chemise with laced ruff- narrow black belt- 16th C. Italian

boy in gray figured silk tunic- undersleeves and border black silk- white lawn puffs- red cap- red cloth stockings- black shoes- Italian- late 15th C.

baby in colored flannel dress over a linen chemise- 16th C. Dutch

little girl in silk frock- puffed sleeves- ruching- girdle with pomander- 16th C. Italian

little girl in blue and red- bodice red- skirt azure blue- yoke, ruff and apron of white lawn- "housewife" on chain girdle- German- 16th C.

little girl in multicolored knitted tabard- scarlet frock- cloth stockings- leather shoes- Dutch- 16th C.

boy in satin of light color- tied slashings over color, probably scarlet- stockings of scarlet cloth- slashed leather shoes- 16th C. Italian

satin gown- sleeves with triple puffs- earrings- necklace- girdle with pomander- Italian- 16th C.

R T W

Seventeenth Century

all-white costume-lace cap-laced collar and cuffs-apron-orange crochet or braid necklace-"housewife" basket with black velvet ribbon-fitted bodice-manteau back-Dutch

boy in rose-colored velvet frock-collar, puffs, frills and bibbed apron of sheer linen-ribbon bands on skirt-toy ornaments-Spanish

jacket, breeches, stockings, shoes, rosettes ginger brown-white silk puffs-embroidered lawn collar and cuffs-felt hat-English

boy-red frock-sleeves of red braid-white puffs-collar, undersleeves, apron and bodice white linen-cap of lace and linen-English

little girl-remains of hanging sleeves-silk frock with wings-lawn and lace underblouse with Medici collar-béret cap with ostrich-Dutch

little girl of the "people"-silk or cloth dress with draped overskirt (manteau)-fontange headdress of lawn and lace-white apron-French

doublet with wings and tabs-"full slops"-linen whisk and cuffs-felt or silk hat-English

English-long coat and waistcoat-embroidery-black velvet breeches-lawn shirt and cravat-black shoes with red heels

a princess-azure blue moiré gown-manteau back-Vandyke lace-apron of silk tissue-English

RTW

Eighteenth Century

little boy in amber satin dress-lingerie cap, frills, cuffs and under sleeves-1st half of C.

cloth coat-black velvet breeches-white linen shirt-black felt tricorne-mid C.

little girl in negligee dress-capelet with pleated frill-fitted, boned bodice-skirt over hoops-mid C.

flowered chintz-lingerie cap, sleeves, neckerchief and apron with lace-1740

boy-silk coat dress-embroidered velvet sash-lingerie shirt-1760

"sailor's trousers"-lingerie blouse-crushed silk or velvet sash-flat soled slippers-1790's

black taffeta calash-collapsible hood on hoops-black taffeta cape edged black lace-1770's

cloth coat-black velvet breeches-linen shirt with long, slim cravat-1730

fine muslin and lace-colored ribbon sash-1780's

RTW

Nineteenth Century—
First Half

mourning dress for little girl—black cashmere—white frills—white mull cap—black ribbon—dark stockings—probably gray—1809

percale frock with eyelet embroidery—silk sash tied in back—corded silk bonnet with taffeta frills—cloth shoes laced on the inner side—1803

jumper suit of brown linen or kerseymere—white cambric collar and frills—white cap with black visor—black pumps—white socks—1806

teen-age boy—dark blue frockcoat—Brandenburg fastenings—gray cloth trousers—blue or black silk topper—1838

small boy in white dress—tunic and pantalons—dark blue embroidery—1826

boy in navy blue tunic—leg-o'-mutton sleeves—pearl buttons—brown trousers—black shoes—1840

boy's sailor suit of white duck or cotton twill—navy blue collar with braid—black silk neckerchief—black hat—1850

dark blue suit with vest and trousers—stiff collar—blue silk tie—1840

Scotch dress with blue bonnet for small boy—pleated skirt—socks and sandals—1840's

R.T.W.

Nineteenth Century
Second Half

"Bloomer"
dress of
silk or
linen-
cord girdle
with
tassels-
1851

boy's Highland
dress-tartan-
doublet-kilt-
sporran of
badger-
Glengarry
bonnet
with sprig
of heather
1854

boy's dress-Russian
style-embroidered
tunic-lingerie under-
blouse-striped ticking
trousers-cloth cap-
leather visor-1854

woolen coat-
wadded border-
pleated bonnet-
black shoes and
stockings-1870's

black velvet with
needlepoint lace-
fringed red silk
sash-black lisle
stockings-black
pumps-silver buckles-
from Little Lord
Fauntleroy-1880's

frock of silk
mull and lace-
rose silk sash-
Kate Greenaway
Birthday
Book-1880's

bustle
silhouette-
fitted bodice-
short cape-
felt hat
with
ostrich-
black
shoes and
stockings-
1885

dress of
striped flannel-
straw hat
with ribbon
and flowers-
black shoes
and socks-
1891

"Eton" suit
dark blue or
black velveteen-
white muslin
blouse and eyelet
embroidery-satin
tie-black shoes
and stockings-
1890's

RTW

Twentieth Century Girls

chambray rompers—lace edged collar and cuffs—square of smocking—1919

all navy blue and white—béret, sweater and flannel skirt 1927

white sweater—blue and white skirt—white straw hat—blue band—blue socks—white shoes—2nd decade

chambray bloomer dress—white collar and cuffs—ric rac braid—1925

wool plaid "baby bunting" self-fringed slide fastener—1939

blue tweed suit—dusty pink sweater—stitched cloth hat—1936

black or green velveteen bolero—pleated plaid skirt—white piqué blouse—velveteen tam with feather—white-socks—white shoes—1939

blue pinafore over striped chambray frock—white piqué collar—ric rac braid—1940

natural cotton gabardine "shortie"—water repellent—lined and collared with wool pile—1945

christening coat and cap—white silk crêpe and lace—china silk lining—cotton flannel interlining—1950's

polka dot cotton sunsuit—shirred on elastic—1950's

Twentieth Century Boys

blue serge suit jacket and bloomers-wool plaid cap-black shoes and stockings-1st decade

plaid flannel tunic suit-white flannel dickey-silk scarf-black patent leather Breton sailor-black shoes and stockings-1st decade

tweed Norfolk suit-black stockings and shoes-1st decade

"Buster Brown" suit of striped woolen cloth-tunic and bloomers-stiff collar-silk scarf-black cloth top shoes-1st decade

mackinaw-heavy cloth-plaid or camel hair color-felt Alpine hat-brown breeches-shoes and stockings-2nd decade

navy or gray flannel Eton suit-Eton cap-stiff collar-1950's

gray or brown woolen suit-jacket, vest and trousers-1920's

navy denim dungarees or blue jeans-checked cotton shirt-1950's

tweed suit-jacket, vest and knickerbockers camel's hair cap-tan calfskin shoes-1930's

snow-suit-cotton poplin-wind and water repellent-collar and lining alpaca wool-slide fastner-navy, brown or green-1950's

Jacquard-patterned sweater with woolen slacks-1950's

RTW

BIBLIOGRAPHY

BIBLIOGRAPHY

AMERICAN INDIANS

The New World—Sixteenth Century Contemporary Writings and Drawings—Edited and Annotated by Stephen Lorant—New York, 1946

The George Catlin Indian Gallery—Smithsonian Institution, Washington, D.C., 1887

Indian Biography—B. B. Thatcher—2 Vols.—New York, 1900

North American Indians—George Catlin—2 Vols.—Edinburgh, Scotland—1926

The League of the Iroquois—Lewis H. Morgan—2 Vols.—New York, 1901

Indians of America—Lillian Davids Fazzini—Wisconsin, 1935

The Book of Indians—Holling C. Holling—New York, 1935

Costume Throughout the Ages—Mary Evans, A. M.—Philadelphia, 1938

Indian Costumes in the United States—Charles Wissler—New York, 1940

Feathers in a Dark Sky—Ray Wilcox—New York, 1941

Aztecs of Mexico—George Valliant—New York, 1944

Nation's Heritage—New York, 1949

Red Jacket—Last of the Seneca—Arthur C. Parker—New York, 1952

Indians of the Americas—National Geographic Society, Washington, D.C.—1955

Indians—American Heritage—New York, 1961

The Concise Encyclopedia of Archaeology—Leonard Cottrell—New York, 1960

MILITARY

Histoire du Costume en France—J. Quicherat—Paris, 1875

Encyclopedia of Costume—James Robinson Planché—London, 1876

Vie Militaire au Moyen Age et la Renaissance—Paul Lacroix—Paris, 1877

Le Costume Chez les Peuples Anciens et Modernes—Fr. Hottenroch—1884

Le Costume Historique—M. A. Racinet—6 Vols.—Paris, 1888

Uniforms of the United States Army—H. A. Ogden and Henry Loomis Nelson—Washington, D.C., 1890

203

FIVE CENTURIES OF AMERICAN COSTUME

The Centennial of the United States Military Academy at West Point,
N.Y.—1802 to 1902—2 Vols. pub. Washington, D.C., 1904

The British Tar in Fact and Fiction—Commander Charles N. Robinson, R.N.—London, 1909

Arms and Armor—Metropolitan Museum of Art—New York, 1911

The Boy's Book of Famous Regiments—H. A. Ogden—New York, 1914

Arms and Armor—Metropolitan Museum of Art—New York, 1915

Notes on Arms and Armor—Metropolitan Museum of Art—New York, 1916

The Kentucky Rifle—Captain John G. W. Dillon—Washington, D.C., 1924

National Geographic Magazine—1925 to 1960's—Washington, D.C.

Uniforms of the American, British, French and German Armies—Charles M. Lefferts—New York, 1926

Histoire du Costume—Jacques Ruppert—Paris, 1930

A Short History of Costume and Armor—Kelly and Schwab—London, 1931

Das Ehrenkleid des Soldaten—Martin Lezius—Berlin, 1936

Adventures of America 1857 to 1900—John A. Kouwenhoven—New York, 1938

Uniforms of the British Army—Cecil C. P. Lawson—2 Vols.—London, 1940

Soldiers of the American Army—1775 to 1954—Fritz Kredel and Frederick P. Todd—Chicago, 1941

Album of American History—James Truslow Adams—4 Vols.—New York, 1944

Hand Cannon to Automatic—Herschel C. Logan—West Virginia, 1944

British Military Uniforms—James Laver—London, 1948

Ciba Review—Military Uniforms—Gessler and Schneider—Basle, Switzerland, 1952

Picture History of the United States Navy—Theodore Roscoe and Fred Freeman—New York, 1956

The American Heritage Picture History of the Civil War—Bruce Catton—New York, 1960

Regiments at a Glance—Lt. Col. Frank Wilson—Canada, 1960

Great American Guns—Will Bryant—New York, 1961

A History of Firearms—Harold L. Peterson—New York, 1961

BIBLIOGRAPHY

HISTORY

The New World—Sixteenth Century Contemporary Writings and Drawings—Edited and annotated by Stephen Lorant—New York, 1946

The Story of the Greatest Nations—Edward S. Ellis and Charles F. Horne, M.S., Ph.D.—10 Vols.—New York, 1901

Harmsworth History of the World—10 Vols.—London, 1907

Encyclopedia Britannica—11th Edition—New York, 1910

National Geographic Magazine—1925 to 1960's—Washington, D.C.

Funk and Wagnalls New Standard Encyclopedia—New York and London, 1931

Album of American History—James Truslow Adams—4 Vols.—New York, 1944

I Remember Distinctly—Agnes Rogers and Frederick Lewis Allen—New York, 1947

The Conquest of Culture—M. D. C. Crawford—New York, 1948

Pioneer America—Carl W. Drepperd—New York, 1949

Women Are Here to Stay—Agnes Rogers—New York, 1949

Life In America—Marshall B. Davidson—2 Vols.—New York, 1951

Divided We Fought—1861-1865—David McDonald—New York, 1952

The New Dictionary of American History—Michael Martin and Leonard Gelber—New York, 1952

Year's Pictorial History of America—California, 1954

The Look of the Old West—Foster-Harris—New York, 1955

American Military History 1607 to 1958—Headquarters, Department of the Army, Washington, D.C., 1959

The American Heritage Picture History of the Civil War—Bruce Catton—New York, 1960

The Concise Encyclopedia of Archaeology—Leonard Cottrell—New York, 1960

Life Magazine—Great Battles of the Civil War—New York, 1961

CIVIL COSTUME

Costumes Anciens et Modernes—Cesare Vecellio—2 Vols.—1590—French Translation, Paris, 1859

Costume in England—F. W. Fairholt—London 1846—Revised 1916

Encyclopedia of Costume—James Robinson Planché—London, 1876

XVIIᵉ Siècle—Institutions, Usages et Costumes—Paul Lacroix—Paris, 1891

The Eighteenth Century—France 1700-1789—Paul Lacroix—Paris, 1876

205

Directoire, Consular et Empire—Paul Lacroix—Paris, 1884

Le Costume Chez les Peuples Anciens et Modernes—Fr. Hottenroth—
  1884

Little Lord Fauntleroy—Frances Hodgson Burnett—New York, 1886

Kate Greenaway Birthday Book—London, 1886

Le Costume Historique—M. A. Racinet—6 Vols.—Paris, 1888

Customs and Fashions in Old New England—Alice Morse Earle—New
  York, 1893

Two Centuries of Costume in America—Alice Morse Earle—New York,
  1894

Child Life in Colonial Days—Alice Morse Earle—New York, 1899

Home Life in Colonial Days—Alice Morse Earle—New York, 1899

Godey's Lady's Book—Magazine—1830 to 1898—Philadelphia

Peterson's Magazine—1840 to 1898—Philadelphia

Social New York Under the Georges—Esther Singleton—New York,
  1902

Die Trachten der Völker—Albert Kretschmer—Leipzig, 1906

Münchner Bilderbogen, Zur Geschichte des Kostums—Braun und
  Schneider—Munich, late 19th century

English Costume—Dion Clayton Calthrop—London, 1907

A Dictionary of Men's Wear—William Henry Baker—New York, 1908

Dutch New York—Esther Singleton—New York, 1909

British Costume During XIX Centuries—Mrs. Charles H. Ashdown—
  London, 1910

Le Costume Civil en France du XIIIᵉ au XIXᵉ Siècle—Camille Piton—
  Paris, 1913

History of Everyday Life in Britain 1066 to 1799—M. and C. H. B.
  Quennell—London, 1918

Life and Work of the People of England—16th Century—Hartley and
  Elliot—London, 1925

Life and Work of the People of England—17th Century—Hartley and
  Elliott—London, 1928

Historic Costume—Kelly and Schwab—London, 1929

Early American Costume—Warwick and Pitz—New York, 1929

Mr. Currier and Mr. Ives—Russel Crouse—New York, 1930

English Children's Costume—Iris Brooke and James Laver—London,
  1930

English Costume—14th through 19th Centuries—Iris Brooke and James
  Laver—New York, 1937

BIBLIOGRAPHY

Costume Throughout the Ages—Mary Evans, A.M.—Philadelphia, 1938

Historic Costume For the Stage—Lucy Barton—New York, 1938

The Language of Fashion—Mary Brooks Picken—New York, 1939

Accessories of Dress—Lester and Oerke—Peoria, Illinois, 1940

Ciba Review—Children's Dress—A. Varron—April 1940—Basle, Switzerland

History of American Costume—Elizabeth McClellan—New York, 1904 and 1942

This Is Fashion—Elizabeth Burris-Meyers—New York, 1943

Pacemakers of Progress—Harold B. Quimby—Chicago, 1946

Everyday Things in American Life—William Chauncy Langdon—2 Vols.—New York, 1946 and 1948

Dictionnaire du Costume—Maurice Leloir—Paris, 1951

The Look of the Old West—Foster-Harris—New York, 1955

Ciba Review—Men's Dress—H. Schramm—January 1958—Basle, Switzerland

A Pageant of Hats, Ancient and Modern—Ruth Edward Kilgour—New York, 1958

The Importance of Wearing Clothes—Lawrence Langer—New York, 1959

ART BOOKS

The Child in Painting—Myrtle D. McGraw—New York, 1941

Folk Art—Alice Ford—New York, 1949

Children in Art—Metropolitan Museum of Art—New York, 1950

Children's Portraits—Bettina Hürlimann—New York, 1950

Child Portraiture—F. M. Godfrey—London, 1956

PERIODICALS

Vogue

Harper's Bazaar

Fashion Digest

Fairchild Publications

Ciba Review, Switzerland

Gentleman's Quarterly

Time

Life

New York Times

New York Herald Tribune